Bouncer

The Geoff Thompson Story

Part Two

Geoff Thompson

SUMMERSDALE

Summersdale Publishers Ltd
46 West Street
Chichester
West Sussex
United Kingdom
PO19 1RP

www.summersdale.com

Printed and bound in Great Britain by Biddles Ltd.,
Guildford and King's Lynn.

ISBN 1 84024 081 4

The names of some of the people and places in this book
have been changed to protect the guilty.

Other books and videos by Geoff Thompson:

Watch My Back – *A Bouncer's story*

Bouncer (the sequel to **Watch My Back**)

The Pavement Arena
– *Adapting Combat Martial Arts to the Street*

Real Self Defence

Real Grappling

Real Punching

Real Kicking

Weight Training For the Martial Artist

Animal Day – *Pressure Testing the Martial Arts*

Tuxedo Warrior – *Tales of a Mancunian Bouncer*
Cliff Twemlow – Foreword By Geoff Thompson

Fear – the friend of exceptional people
– *Techniques in Controlling Fear*

Dead or Alive – *The Complete Self Protection Handbook*
(as released by Paladin Press in the USA)

Blue Blood on the Mat
Athol Oakley – Foreword Geoff Thompson.

The Ground Fighting series:
Vol One – Pins, the bedrock
Vol Two – Escapes
Vol Three – Chokes and Strangles
Vol Four – Arm bars and Locks
Vol Five – Fighting from neutral knees
Vol Six – Fighting from your back

Videos – (all videos one hour approx)

Lessons with Geoff Thompson:
Animal Day – *Pressure Testing the Martial Arts*
Animal Day Part 2, *A Deeper Look – The Fights*

Three Second Fighter – *The Sniper Option*

The Ground Fighting series:
Vol One – Pins, the bedrock
Vol Two – Escapes
Vol Three – Chokes and strangles
Vol Four – Bars and joint locks
Vol Five – Fighting from neutral knees
Vol Six – Fighting from your back

Forthcoming books:
Real Head, Knees and Elbows
Contemporary Self Protection
(released as *Dead or Alive* in USA)

About The Author

Geoff Thompson has written over twenty published books and is known world wide for his autobiographical books charting nine years working as a nightclub doorman, *Watch My Back*, *Bouncer* and *On The Door*. He holds the rank of 5th Dan black belt in Japanese karate, 1st Dan in Judo and is also qualified to senior instructor level in various other forms of wrestling and martial arts. He has several scripts for stage, screen and T.V. in development with Destiny Films.

He has published several articles for GQ magazine, and has also been featured in FHM, Maxim, Arena, Front and Loaded magazines, and has appeared many times on mainstream T.V.

Geoff is currently a contributing editor for Men's Fitness magazine and self-defence columnist for Front.

Violence

You can run, but it will catch you,
You can hide, but it will seek.
You can close your eyes, but when they open it will still
be there.
You can succumb, but then it will devour,
You can cry, but it thrives on tears.
WARNING! WARNING! Violence is now off the
reservation.
Don't run,
Don't hide,
Nor close your eyes,
Do not succumb,
Nor shed tears,
Straighten your spine,
Fix your gaze,
And fight back . . . then, and only then, are you in with a
chance.

G.T.

For my beautiful Sharon

Contents

Preface

'How's work, Ian?' I asked a policeman friend of mine, who was also one of the better students at my karate class.

He frowned,

'Oh busy, really busy.'

'As a copper in Coventry, Ian,' I sympathised, 'you're always going to be busy.'

He feigned a smile, then sighed a deep, 'disappointed' sigh.

'Yeah, what a shit-hole this has turned out to be!'

Foreword

After writing *Watch My Back*, and recalling some of the happenings of my life, I cupboarded the manuscript for a couple of years, mainly due to laziness and lack of direction. After the said two years, I gave it a dusting-down and sent the proposed book to my local paper, 'The Coventry Evening Telegraph', for a professional view. I wasn't sure if it was any good or not. Also I thought an article in the newspaper about myself and the book might help me to attract a publisher.

After a couple of weeks, Sue Lary, a lovely reporter from the paper, arranged to meet me and offer a little advice. She said that she liked the book and agreed to do an article in the newspaper. She also (very kindly) offered me some constructive criticism and advice.

The floodgates opened.

I took home what was to be the skeleton of my new book. I re-wrote it completely adding extra stories and added description. However, in the gap between first writing *Watch My Back* and completion of its publication, I not only remembered other situations from the door, but many more had occurred. So I decided to write a sequel. Here it is. I hope you enjoy it.

I would like to add at this point that I am not a thug, I have never liked violence and have never looked for trouble, though it has followed me around somewhat.

I spend my days trying to be a better person. I ask here as I did at the beginning of *Watch My Back* that you read with an open mind.

Some of the incidents in this book are new, some are old. They are written in the sequence in which I remember them as opposed to the sequence in which they happened. The reason for this is that I am forever remembering – or indeed being reminded of – old incidents whilst at the same time and in the mean time, new incidents are occurring (people just keep attacking me).

To my critics I would ask but one small favour (just fuck off! Only joking), if after reading this book you feel that I have 'sinned', then let he who has not cast the first stone.

1. Choosing

In my time as a doorman I have seen the sad demise of many marriages (my own included). Often when the demands of the job get too much it has a direct affect on the family unit; late nights, mood swings, arguments, pent-up anger and unutilised adrenaline all add to the heavy toll that 'the door' can take. The money that you earn, and any kudos accrued rarely compensates.

Often the pressure forces an ultimatum from one's partner: 'me or the job'. Some give up the job to save the relationship, others choose the company of their mates of the same ilk.

The choice, of course, is a personal one.

R had 'worked' the door most of his life and was married to a lovely girl who had borne him beautiful children, but the door was killing what they had and she had given him an ultimatum on more than one occasion. This time though, she meant it. R had a very big decision to make. If it were just an ordinary job it might have been an easier decision, but the door is no ordinary job, it sucks you into its black hole and holds you like metal to magnet. Breaking away, even when you want to, can be a very difficult, sometimes impossible. Also, your work mates are no ordinary work mates, they are comrades, brothers in arms; the glue-bonded affinity is something akin to love. It can get so close that you start to want to be with them more than your family. This makes the other half feel like second best. This is where the problems usually start and relationships that are a bit frayed around the edges start to fall apart like a cheap suit.

We'd been brought to the N door to clean the place up, like latter-day marshals. The place was an infestation of violence, seeing many of the previous doormen stabbed, slashed, bottled, glassed and threatened with guns, the instigators being the local lowlifes – the Bell Green Boys.

I personally thought they were shit-bags, and was more than prepared, for the right money, to meet them on their own turf.

As it turned out they gave me a wide berth and never used or abused the establishment whilst I was there, it was the older ones, who should really have known better, who decided to 'chance their arm'.

First Mr C (detailed account of the Mr C saga in *Watch My Back*), who never got past the first hurdle, then the bullies from the O up the road, who, it seemed, thought they ruled the proverbial roost. There were too many chiefs and not enough Indians as it turned out!

The O crew were not babies, they were grown men and fearsome men at that. They'd heard (apparently) that I was coming to the N, and resented me putting my pitch on their park. Quite frankly I didn't give a monkey's fuck what they thought. I didn't want trouble with them nor was I about to court it – that was never my way – but on the other hand, nor would I tolerate them 'fucking around' in the N whilst I was being paid to look after it.

I was reliably informed that the previous doormen danced to whatever tune the O crew played, and lived in absolute fear of them. This was not unusual in this blot area on the Coventry map. The O crew had gained respect in the city, but it was respect born through fear, stolen not given. Respect is worthless unless it's earned. Any half-wit can point a loaded gun and demand respect but it brings with it 'hate'. Real respect encourages co-operation and understanding.

Saturday night saw me reclined on a cheap white plastic garden chair. My feet rested wearily on a pigeon shit decorated wooden bench in front of me. With a half lager and a bag of smoky bacon crisps at my side and the warm evening sun on my brow, I remember thinking 'it doesn't get much better than this'. Things were looking good. I'd scared off the fearsome Mr C with comparative ease. Even though he'd threatened to have me shot, I was comfortable in the knowledge that I had made my mark on one of the bigger fish in the manor. The subsequent ripples would warn off any 'minnows' with a taste for conflict.

'You've got a good job, you 'ave.' The unsolicited voice of a local broke my thoughts. I smiled, but didn't answer. They all say that, but when it 'kicks off' they abandon such empty sentiments in their rush for the exit.

R was inside talking to a young lady, and a peppering of people sat around the newly refurbished lounge. The room had a bit of a cold, unwelcome feel to it like a vacant house. Eight thirty p.m., anytime now, the place would start to fill up.

I have to admit I hated the place. I tried to tell myself that it would get better, but I knew it wouldn't. Philosophically speaking, I knew that you couldn't put a shine on a piece of crap, but could only learn to endure the stench. The problem was that I'd moved from a lovely little number in the 'Dip' (Diplomat), to the N because I needed the extra money and they'd offered. They'd smartened the place up quite nicely, but the words 'shine' and 'crap' weren't going to be erased by a bit of paint and wall paper. It's people that make slums.

I had made a lot of friends in the locals whom, I think, saw me as their knight, someone to slay the fire-breathing dragons of the manor.

R was still giving his 'knicker-loosening lecture' to the young lady by the bar, when he was rudely interrupted by a hard-faced, black-moustached man to his left. He was a scruffy fucker in dire need of a fashion transplant. His dark marble eyes held a look of malice and sheer nastiness. He looked like a mafioso. The locals hated him because of his bullying ways. Shadowing him was a giant of a man with stony diarrhoea-inducing eyes that had most people 'shitting themselves' at fifty yards. His gait was totally uncompromising. He weighed in at an impressive sixteen stone but looked as though he might have problems stringing sentences together.

R didn't know it at the time, but these two were leaders of the O crew, here to show us who and what they were – though it took a belly full of beer for them to summon the courage. They needn't have bothered, I could see right from the off what they were – shit-bags. I didn't like either of them, nor what they stood for. The onlookers murmured in quietened expectation, stomachs churning, they'd seen this movie before.

The mafioso approached R, mouth grimacing, face screwed up like chewed toffee. 'Why are you such a big-headed wanker?'

R's eyes widened as they left the pretty frame of the 'arm candy'. He was dumbfounded. He quickly tried to collect himself, he had been hit by an adrenal dump.

Adrenaline comes in many ways, this being the most dangerous of all. It hits you so quickly that there's very little time to control it. If you see it coming you can mentally prepare yourself, but if it blindsides you the reasoning process mistakes the feeling for fear and you're frozen in the face of ensuing danger.

'What?' R replied, his fleshy jowls shuddering under the weight of the fear.

This is the second that most fighters dread, the last second before battle when you know it's gonna kick off and you want to be anywhere else in the world but where it's at. When your knees do an involuntary Bossanova, your mouth dries up like an old sock, your ears blank out everything but the voice of the antagonist and your eyes tunnel. Every doubt about your ability to 'handle it' jams your 'switch board' and romanticised ideas about fighting disappear like hoovered dust.

BANG!

The mafioso fired a head butt into his face. R, more than a little stunned, grabbed his attacker around the neck, pulled him close and bit a hole in his face (R was like that). The shadowy man of stone, seeing his friend's dilemma, joined in on the attack.

'GEOFF!' The loud shout made me jump out of a daydream where I was back at the Diplomat surrounded by the warmth of familiarity.

'Are you working tonight, or what? R's getting battered in there.'

It was Gez, my bespectacled friend whose large nose had its own orbital system, it was mapped in the local A-Z. It was…a big nose. I leapt from my seat sending it tumbling to the ground and ran into R's aid. My half-eaten bag of Walkers tumbled to the ground scattering my snack across the floor. I just hoped that the crisp thief Garry Lineker was not in the vicinity.

The two men were swinging off R's neck like scarves. As soon as I clapped eyes on them I knew who they were, what they were, and what was occurring. This was an attempt at stamping their authority, letting us know that they were in charge. They could find no legitimate excuse for fighting with us, so, plied with drink, they'd started an affray for nothing. I felt a nervous apprehension as I approached. I felt as though I was moving in slow motion. I knew we were about to destroy these wankers, I also knew that it was going to start a war. They were heavy and had been known to introduce 'lead' on more than one occasion. The mafioso was the younger brother of one of Coventry's most famous fighters, and didn't he tear the arse out of it. Everywhere he went, every fight he fought it was, 'do you know who my brother is?' or, 'I'll bring my brother down here'.

His brother was a face, he was a hard man, but that didn't give him the right to go around beating people up or intimidating them in his brother's name. His brother wouldn't always be there . . . he wasn't there that night (ha ha).

I'd heard many, many stories of the fighting prowess of his brother Baz, but I didn't care. I didn't doubt the validity of these stories but I also knew that he was a fair person, a gentleman, and wouldn't go fighting his brother's battles when he was 'out of order'.

R was struggling to fight off his assailants so I reached up and grabbed 'Stone-face' by the shoulder pulling him free from R. As I did so, he turned and threw his right fist in the general direction of my nose. Lack of speed betrayed him and I quickly pulled his left shoulder with my right hand forcing his face into three fierce left uppercuts. The sound of knuckle on face echoed in the smoke-filled room. He was in dreamsville. As he lay helpless at my feet several boots from the crowd that had now gathered around us shot into his unresponsive body with resounding grunts and thuds. The sounds of violence, of splitting skin and breaking bones were sickening. Stone-face had always been an instrument of pain to these amicable locals, the disembodied kicks lay recompense for this. I looked across just in time to see a bloody mafioso scuttling cravenly out of the exit door. He had left his mate at our mercy and his bottle in a steaming trail behind him. R had disappeared behind the bar. I turned to see Stone-face rising bewildered from his bed on the dance floor. Everyone moved away from him. Still scared but in control, I lined him up with a right to take him out again. This time I'd make sure he stayed down till the paramedics arrived. He was by reputation a nasty fucker, so I could afford him no chances.

'You've got to leave mate,' I told him, the adrenaline pushing an embarrassing shake into my voice. He nodded but there was a lack of congruence with his eyes that said 'maybe I'll go for it'. At the same time he searched the room for mafioso. I admired him for not wanting to leave without first checking his whereabouts and safety, obviously not knowing that mafioso had broken the four minute mile and was probably in the city centre by now.

'You've got to leave,' I said again, but had a big right in the wings to back it up this time. I took in a deep breath through my nose to steady my voice and add a little more authority. He stared at me and for just a second I thought I saw a glint of fight left in his eyes, but I guess it was just a piece of shit off the dance floor, because he turned and began to leave.

Just as we got to the door and he was about to go I felt a rush of wind 'whoosh' past my head.

BANG!

R was back from behind the bar with a baseball bat and bad intention. He let rip with all his might and smashed it right into the back of Stone-face's head. A sickly, hollow thud echoed across the room and the whole of his body lurched forward with the impact. The connection of bat on skull sounded like a hammer on a paving slab. My eyes shot around to see R. He had an 'out of control', angry, crazy look on his face as he swung the bat again and again at the now, understandably, cowering man before him. He managed to scramble outside, trying to protect his head. R was close on his trail. As R leathered his fourth shot into Stone-face, I thought it about time I intervened to stop the slaughter. I jumped on R's back, unfortunately just as he was retracting the bat for his fifth home run. The bat whacked me on the head but luckily it only stopped me for an eight count. I held R tightly around the neck to try to stop him hammering Stone-face into the ground like a tent peg. R, being twenty stone, and me being a mere lightweight at thirteen stone, he threw me around like a flag. I was a jumper on a windy clothes-line. After what seemed like a lifetime I finally managed to stop the onslaught, probably saving Stone-face's life. R pounded angrily back inside and Stone-face hobbled off in the general direction of the O, holding on to his head like it was about to fall off. He didn't look quite so menacing now; in fact he looked pitiful.

R's anger was still not assuaged. In the bar he paced around like a wounded bear.

'Where's the other wanker, the one who nutted me?' he shouted.

Then he ran, still wielding the bat, through the lounge and into the toilets in hot pursuit of mafioso. I ran after him again to make sure he didn't do too much damage.

The communal troughs lay empty. 'Thank fuck for that,' I thought.

One of the two cubicles was locked though, obviously occupied. R kicked open the flimsy door to reveal a skinny, trembling, bespectacled man sat on the toilet, his trousers around his ankles. He was not our man, though I suspect he had just found an immediate cure for constipation. It was a close encounter of the turd kind. I was glad, it would have been a messy job.

We closed the broken door and went back to the lounge, where I finally managed to calm R down.

Lance, the bespectacled manager, had absolutely the wrong temperament for pub management. He approached us nervously.

'Do you know who they were?'

We both looked at him. I knew, though it was obvious that R didn't, because when Lance told him, he went pale. Lance, I've got to say, was a spineless bastard who didn't even have the dignity to try to hide his sheer and absolute panic. The trouble with panic is, when openly displayed, it becomes highly contagious, and everyone in close proximity to 'Whimpering Lance' seemed to be coming down with it, and running around in a frenzy.

I kept myself calm, though I could feel the extreme strain of panic trying to crack my will. I fought against it with the army of my self-control. I said very little.

'They'll be back,' said one.

'Get out of it Geoff, they're too heavy,' said another.

They were all trying to worry monger me, but I wasn't having any of it. I picked my words carefully in answer to their statements.

'Let them come, I'm not going anywhere.'

I wanted to though. I wanted to go home, far away from it all. I wished it hadn't happened, and that I wasn't involved, but it had and I was, so (I told myself) 'shut the fuck up and get on with it!'

I can be very hard on myself at times.

In this job you learnt all about fear, you also learnt to expect its company. This was the third and most corrosive form of adrenaline, and probably the one that stayed longest and tested your resolve the most. This is mostly due to its absolute surprise; I am talking about the adrenaline of aftermath. Win or lose, this 'will executioner' arrives and floods you with anticipation. The worry mongers who feel it is their absolute duty to remind you of the shit you are in perpetuate it. The key with this baby is expectancy.

After every battle I mentally prepare myself for its arrival. If you expect a blow then its impetus is greatly reduced. Though it can still be a bastard you can control it more easily when you see it coming. I've witnessed the retirement of many good doormen due to aftermath.

'Do you think I was over the top, Geoff? With the bat I mean.'

R's voice sounded shaky, his face held a worried hue. He didn't want to be here either. I was blunt.

'Yeah, you were over the top R. But don't worry about it, because it's done. There's nothing we can do about it now.'

R and I were on our own. The two other doormen that worked with us didn't want to know – it was all too much for them. I didn't blame them. Oh, I know I should have been offended but when it's gone it's gone. And anyway, it's their prerogative. Only a decision – stay or go – stands between the hero and the coward. Some stay and become legends; others go and probably never forgive themselves, even though perhaps others do. It does leave you in the shit though.

Lance was still running around like a headless chicken, spouting on about how we were all doomed. Excited, frightened chatter spread through the room which was emptying by the minute.

Then worry mongers began their work.

Every time I turned around some spoon wanted to tell me what grave danger I was in, trying to frighten me off, dying to see the arse fall out of my trousers. I stuck to my one liner and told everyone the same thing. 'If they want to fight, I'm here. They can come, I'm going nowhere.'

I'm always careful of what I say and how I act when the heat is on, because when it's all over every single word will be remembered, recalled and recounted like a bad film. Better to be remembered for strong words than weak ones.

A huge, fat, bearded man who must have got his underpants on prescription, walked past me on his way to the exit. He stopped briefly beside me and whispered:

'There are thirty of them on the way down, and they've got guns.'

A rush of adrenaline shot through my body as he spoke. I fought to control it, but it was running riot. I hid it, never let it show. You can't show any weakness.

'Fuck this,' said R.

'Shut the doors, shut the doors,' shouted Lance hysterically.

Somebody locked the front doors. R picked up his baseball bat from behind the bar where he had left it in a bucket of cold water to cool down. I took a 'steel fist' out of my pocket. Tony looked at the steel and smiled, I smiled back. We were ready.

I put my mind into top gear. When they crashed down the doors I was going to hit anything that moved, fight till I dropped, and anyone who touched me was going to 'have some'. I might well lose I figured, but I was going to take teeth and flesh with me. If these people wanted to dance, then play the music and let's dance.

With the doors closed the room took on a sombre air. Silhouetted figures moved eerily around the room. A bad smell of anticipation hovered in the air. I heard shouting coming from outside. R's face gave an involuntary shiver and his eyes locked on to the space by the front door. He gripped the bat so tightly that his knuckles went white. He shook the bat as though readying for a fast ball; we became oblivious to everything else in the room, locked in one of those long moments, ready for battle. Nothing and no one else existed. For those few seconds before there seemed to be nothing else in the world but that door and us. The fear had gone now, and had been replaced by an acceptance of 'what will be'. In those bonding seconds there was a marrying of spirits, a camaraderie that'd have us locked in brotherhood for eternity.

CRASH! CRASH! CRASH!

The windows smashed, spitting glass this way and that. My eyes never left the closed front door for what was an houred second. My fist clenched tightly around the cold steel of my 'duster. I winked cheekily at R.

'I think we've upset them.'

He smiled back 'you mad bastard'. He lifted his bat like an axe-man at an oak, in baited anticipation for the inevitable. This was it.

CRASH! CRASH!

More exploding windows. We waited, eyes locked on the doors, ready now. The room was a flask of frightened screams that never seemed to reach our ears.

'THEY'VE GONE,' a disembodied voice shouted, piercing the adrenaline-induced deafness. A thousand relieved sighs rolled through the room. The anxiety remained. I knew that this little episode was only the beginning, it was far from over. I knew; I'd been here before.

Lance 'the wimp' went straight back into his 'dance of the headless chicken' routine. He looked at every broken window as though it were antique and cradled every broken piece. He moaned and whimpered and I despised him for being so unashamedly blatant about it, not so much because I didn't like cowards, after all we all have a coward in us, rather it was that I found his weakness unnerving, almost infectious.

'Shut your fucking mouth, it's only glass,' I told him.

That did the trick.

My bed blankets were nettles. I tossed and turned running the night's happenings over and again in my mind. Studying and analysing, looking at it from every conceivable angle and then again, like a complex equation that demanded an answer, but seemed not to hold one. I recalled my decimation of Stone-face and how surprisingly easy it had been. I was surprised. His 'rep' was big and he'd taken out many fighters that I personally rated. Perhaps he was just on a bad night – we all have them. Or maybe it was the beer; perhaps I was just lucky (NO WAY!), or perhaps karma was paying a visit to the N that night. Either way, it was definitely not one of his better days. The consolation of my victory over Stone-face was still not enough to buy me any sleep. Even as I left the pub that evening, I knew that sleep would elude me, it always did in times of high stress. It was a part of the toll that this kind of life exacted. My only real consolation was the fact that I knew I wasn't the only one who would be losing sleep. After all, I hadn't had my reputation shimmied all over the N dance floor like a cleaners mop. I didn't throw the gauntlet with all my might and get a spanking for my troubles. If (I surmised) I was lying on a bed of nettles then others must surely be sharing a similar fate.

The next day phone calls were made, many phone calls. A show of strength was needed. Actually a fucking army was needed. But it wasn't a problem, my friends were many and everyone asked would come to my aid.

The N was a mere knife's throw from the infamous Bell Green, where violence was more common than fish and chips, and faces, craft-knifed and Stanleyed, were in abundance. Severed ears, the result of venomous battles, were worn as prizes on key rings. If the ear had been cut or bitten off the head of a name fighter it would be auctioned in the pubs to the highest bidder. The unfortunates who lost an ear forever afterwards were the brunt of unsolicited jokes:

'Can I get you a pint?'

'No thanks, I've got one 'ear!'

Inside the N the lounge was full to capacity with doormen, between forty and fifty of us, all told, with not a weak link in sight. Everyone could and would go the distance, everyone a rook or a knight or a king, no pawns in this crowd. Every fighter in the room was 'the man' in his own particular area of the city.

Tracy, from Wyken, short, with cropped light hair (courtesy of Winson Green) and a hard, scarred face. He was tough and uncompromising, a wizard with a baseball bat.

'Ginger' John, also small in height, though very large in stature. Diminutively innocent-looking face, but held faultless 'hands' and a cast iron will. Nicknamed 'Horlicks' by his fellow doormen, because he always put people to 'sleep' last thing at night.

'No Neck' Maynard, no neck, and no heart.

'Awesome' Anderson, who quite simply was.

Ricky 'Jabber' James, the towering seventeen stone Midlands pro-boxing champ.

'Killer' Kilbane, if his cripple shooting right never put you to sleep, his vignettes of past battles would.

Kev, he was a gentleman, but from his alter-ego issued a psychotic fighter who ruled the unruleable Willenhall with unpretentious certainty.

'Wicked' Winston, whose 'people pummeling' hands etched themselves into the brow and memory of everyone unfortunate to have 'stopped' them.

'Sheffield' Jonny. Liked to 'carry'. Legend has it that he once tripped and fell, stabbing himself six times.

And more, many more. I was the proud host of the greatest assembled 'team' ever to stand together in one room.

R approached me. His cigarette trembled as he put it to the match. His robust, scarred face capped by dark and smartly parted short hair, looked tired and worried. His eyes betrayed him. The pressure, I knew, was getting to him.

He kept an even look on his face, to hide his fear, it was hidden from most, but to me it stood out like a bulldog's bollocks. I hated to see him this way.

'I don't need all this,' he said quietly, 'I never slept a fucking wink last night.'

He wandered off and made polite conversation with our guests.

John 'Awesome' Anderson approached me. He stood straight-backed and confident at five foot eight, his skin caramel. To the uninitiated he looked mean and unwelcoming, and why not – he was.

'Where are they then?' he asked, squinting his eyes and slowly drawing on his cigarette. I shrugged my shoulders. It was nine thirty p.m. and our sparring partners had not yet arrived.

We'd had it on good authority that the O crew had planned a return visit for tonight. They had sent a few spies down to see what kind of fire-power we were holding. The returned reports must have put the shits up them, because they never left the safety of the O.

'I'm sick of this fucking waiting,' said John. 'We'll send a scout party down there to see what's keeping them.' John wasn't one to hang around; he'd fought that many battles that the locals had called him 'one man gang'.

At this, John, Colin, Ricky, Winston, Paul and Big Neil sauntered off to the O and entered a very unwelcoming bar. The crowded room fell silent, except for the confident banter of 'Kamikaze' John, and the boys who laughed and joked with each other. There is nothing more intimidating than walking into an opponent's lair and displaying blatant fearlessness. The O crew had never experienced such a display of courage. It scared them; they were only used to giving it out.

When he found out that the lads had gone up to the O, Lance was, to say the least, not happy and he told me so.

'I never told them to go up, they went of their own accord,' I said. I looked closely at this portly, middle-aged man and wondered what the fuck he was doing in a trade like this. He'd have been better suited to managing a supermarket. Basically, he was a nice man in the wrong job, and the stress must have been taking years off his life, it certainly was off mine.

When the lads returned, they were in good spirits. They couldn't believe that these so-called hard men had let them, so few in number, in and out of their local unchallenged.

'Wankers,' John, the man of few words concluded. I had to agree.

Last time the O crew had trouble (with the doormen before us), they had turned up in large numbers with hand guns and made the doormen get on their knees and beg. They didn't seem too keen now that the odds were a little more even.

The rest of the night, not surprisingly, went without incident. If it was going to happen it would have been tonight, I told myself. Of course, the locals said and kept saying 'they'll be back, and soon', and because I was the head doorman I was the one that was going to 'suffer'.

'They do house visits you know,' a kind, informative, worry-mongering local told me, 'they got one chap in his house, beat up his wife, locked the kids in another room then pummelled him to fuck. Beat him so much that he pissed and shit himself, spewed blood, and was in a coma for ages.'

'Is that right?' I said, pretending that I didn't give a fuck, hiding the fear the words instilled in me. I think that this nondescript, worm of a man was hinting that I was going to get a home visit.

'Hey, don't you have a wife and kids?'

'They can knock my door anytime they like, but the bastards will only do it once,' I said, pointing aggressively at my own chest, 'I do house visits as well, and I'm not the only one around here with a wife and kids. Tell them from me that I'm ready when they are!'

I threw the words at him like rocks, fucking low life. He backed away in a hurry. In days of old the bearer of bad news was always killed. If he didn't fuck off quick I was going to regress myself back a couple of hundred years and obliterate him.

I did indeed harbour weaknesses, and yes they were trying to break out, but I would never, never let them. I had, through training, and in real combat, hardened and reinforced my will. It'd take more than a shit-cunt like this to crack it.

Another restless night of tossing and turning lay before me, but I could handle it. I have known stress well. We ate together, slept together, worked together and trained together. It was an absolute and utter bastard at times, but you learnt to live with it. Either that or the fucker eats you up. It never goes away, it always hurts, you just learn to not mind that it hurts. It was at times like this that you earned a year's money all at once.

At times – especially when I was tired – nagging doubts about my ability to handle this situation filtered in. Beautiful cooked dinners were force-fed and lay heavy on my stomach. Sex had become an effort. Every time I reached the 'vinegar strokes' the aforementioned threats swam, unchecked into my mind, reducing the whole performance to lack lustre. I promised myself that this would be the last time (for fighting, not sex) and after it was sorted out I'd 'lose the door' for some job less destroying. I'd pull away from this thing called 'violence', become a recluse. Find a gentler way.

What a lot of bollocks!

A few months after it was over I'd be telling my mates about 'the time I cleaned up in the N'. Romanticising the whole shabang to fuck, making out it was all a bit of a wheeze, a little fun. The vignettes totally lacking the cold reality of violence and its soul brother the diarrhoea-inducing fear.

Visualisation was a small escape.

Thud . . . thud . . . thud . . . thud. My fists sank into the canvass of my heavy punch bag. In my mind's eye it was flesh and bone. I watched my antagonists fall to the mighty wrath of my practiced hands.

'Humph, hu-humph.' I buried the drilled kicks into the belly of the bag letting out a chilling, blood curdling 'KIAAAAA'. I was really there. I felt satisfaction as their bodies fell at my feet, grey with unconsciousness, hitting the paving stones with the cold, sickly wallop of a chicken hitting the cutting board. Salty sweat stung as it ran from brow to eyes, my nostrils inflated and deflated like a raging bull, steam rose from my head, my teeth gritted as I sucked in air. I will never give in, NEVER, NEVER!

THUD!

My right fist buried itself deep into the punch bag to underline my resolve. I grabbed the bag and bit hard into it like I was tearing off a nose, spit and snot splattering everywhere. I was becoming an animal.

Writing this I hardly recognise myself. In retrospect I hate what I had become. But I had to survive.

The thing with pressure is that it flows over into your private life, everything goes on hold until the situation is resolved. Sometimes that can take months. Coping with the pressure leaves you little energy to do anything else, like play with the kids. You also find yourself short-tempered, and who gets it? Those closest to you unfortunately. You want to ask them for help but there is nothing that they can do, nothing anyone can do, and all the time Mr Negative keeps trying to crack you, telling you that 'you can't handle it', 'you're finished', 'give in', 'everyone will understand'. But you learn from experience not to take any shit from anyone, least of all from yourself. If you do he fucks you up badly. Once you allow Mr Negative houseroom he devours you mercilessly. As soon as he comes into my head I fuck him off straight away. I bash him back with positive thoughts or just ignore him like a wiffy smell.

Wednesday night again saw me at the front door of the N, Alan by my side. He wasn't there on the night of the fight, but he was here now. He'd been warned, as had I, that he ought not to fuck with these people, but that was all the more reason for him to stay.

Nine o'clock at night and R hadn't turned up for work yet. I half expected him not to turn up at all. The pressure on him at home didn't help. His wife had given him a choice; the door or her. The choice wasn't quite as simple as it might seem because if he left the job now, in the midst of a crisis it could be seen by others as a bottle-drop, then the reputation he'd spent a lifetime building would be lost. To try to resolve the situation, I had attempted to set up a 'one-on-one' between R and Stone-face. The message returned to me that the situation had gone beyond that – which basically meant they didn't have the balls for a 'straightener'. I was also informed that they had no beef with me, they only wanted R.

This was a mistake on their part really because it showed that their hand was weak, in fact fucking shaky. This just added to my resolve. I sent a message back saying that we were a team, they couldn't have one without the other. Paradoxically I was told from other sources that I, being the head doorman, was going to get my legs blown off.

A bit severe I think you'll agree. And as if that wasn't enough, on Saturday night we were going to get a visit from the petrol bomb wielding Hell's Angels.

R arrived two hours late at ten p.m., there were a few locals enjoying a drink in the lounge. Alan had just nipped to the loo. I sat on my favourite plastic garden chair outside on the patio, enjoying and savouring a lovely half pint of lager and a bag of smoky bacon. He approached looking surprisingly jolly. He bounced up the three steps to where I sat. We exchanged greetings; he apologised for being late. I accepted his apology – we danced!

He wasn't really happy. It was a front. He'd made his choice and had come to tell me.

'Guess what?'

'What?' I replied.

'I've got myself a job as a security man.'

It was a sad moment. I knew what was coming.

'The only trouble is,' he continued, 'it's shifts.'

'Great. So what does that mean exactly?' I asked.

His smile evaporated, his eyes dropped. Where I'd once seen strength in his big face I now saw sadness; unity replaced by confusion. It made me sad. I had always seen R as a Rock, an Island. I knew how he felt because I felt – was feeling – the same.

'Look Geoff, I've been doing this job for fifteen years, I've been there, I've seen it all, but now I've had to make a choice. I need my family and I don't need the door. I'm packing it in.'

He looked up at me and our eyes met. I smiled. A mixture of relief and sadness ran through me.

In a way I was relieved that he was leaving because, selfishly, I knew it would put an end to the war. R knew this too, and I figure that it was partly why he had made this decision. I also felt ashamed at feeling relief.

To me, R leaving the door was an end of an era, he was an institution, untouchable, it shook the very foundations of everything I believed in. The choice he made was a brave one. I admired him. I knew what leaving the job meant to him. I also knew many men who were not brave enough to make that decision, me included.

No one resented R for leaving; in fact Lance nearly wet himself with joy. They all respected his decision. I reached out and put my arms around his huge solid frame and we hugged.

'Just remember R, I love ya.'

He half smiled, 'I know.'

This, of course, was the loop-hole the O were looking for, they wanted a way out that wouldn't lose them too much face and this was it. With R gone they had no reason to fight any more. 'Saturday' threats still came our way though, so minus R, Alan and I manned the door with a duster – not the feather variety of course, that just would not do – and a bat. Not much of a defence against a gun or a petrol bomb I grant you but it was better than nothing.

Saturday night came and went, albeit very slowly, without incident. On the following Tuesday the O crew came to the N when I wasn't there to call a truce with Lance. It was granted. Peace and tranquillity came to the forefront once again. The locals were jubilant because the outcome (as they, I, and everyone else saw it) was a major victory for us.

So, the rats had been led off to the drowning river but manager Lance suddenly decided that he could no longer afford to pay the piper. Now that the danger was gone he thought that he could drop wages and lose doormen.

'Well, we just can't afford to pay you as much now Geoff.'

His whole body shook as he spoke to me, I think he was expecting a dig.

'Hold on a minute Lance, are you telling me that after all the shit we've been through you're gonna drop our money?'

'It's not exactly like that Geoff, just get rid of a couple of the lads, you won't lose any money, there's no reason why you need lose out.'

I shook my head in disgust.

'You should be ashamed of yourself Lance, you're lucky I don't give you a dig. I'll tell you what you can do with your job, you can stick it up your arse-hole.' I walked out of the pub.

Two months after I had left, the pub was once again infested with violence. The door was run by the O crew.

A few months after I left, the N was closed down. It has never opened again since.

Some time later I got to meet Baz (the brother of mafioso) socially. He was one of the toughest, most charismatic men I have ever had the pleasure of meeting. He was also, as I rightly thought, a gentleman.

2. A Hunt for Gold

The rap of brass knocker on porch door echoed through an empty house. Her stomach clenched with apprehension. No reply. She knocked again and stood back so as to get a wider view of the house. Her eyes scanned the Georgian bay-window, then the bedroom windows for signs of life. The doorknocker rattled for the third time. She had to be sure that no one was at home in this modestly detached brick abode. Her calculating beetle-black eyes again checked all windows for signs of life. Black hair hung lankly above and around her much-beaten face, moulded by a multitude of fists. First at the hand of her dad, then her brothers, and now P, who, though villainous, seemed so sweet to her before the wedding that she thought life might be taking a turn for the better. The broken nose he gave her as a wedding present soon put paid to those dreams. Her drab, food-stained attire hung loosely from her frame, a man's suit on a broomstick. The knocked door stayed unanswered. She felt a surge of excitement rush through her body as she walked down the paved entry to the rear garden gate, avoiding the drip, drip of water from the upstairs overflow pipe. The gate, much to her delight, was unlocked.

'Fucking amateurs! Won't they ever learn?'

This house was an early Christmas present, a gift from God. Huge conifer trees to the front and rear ensured seclusion. A neighbouring house was set slightly forward to the left of it, and another set slightly back to the right. Built that way to ensure privacy for the owners, but a godsend for thieves and vagabonds. She kicked through the low-level kitchen window. This was the fourth time she'd robbed this particular house. No burglar alarm, no dogs, no nosy neighbours – happy birthday! It was like collecting dole on a Thursday.

As the glass shattered into the kitchen, the next-door neighbours' dog barked out an alarm and ran to the 'help-the-burglar' six foot fence. She tucked herself back in the entry for a moment, just to make sure the dog wasn't followed by an inquiring master. It wasn't. The fucking dog barked so often that they had learnt to ignore it.

There were four locks on this door, only three of which were in operation. The top inside bolt was not secured, the middle key lock was. So was the switch lock on the door handle and the lower bolt. The lower bolt and switch lock were quickly unfastened leaving only the obstacle of the key lock, which was really no obstacle at all because the owners had left the keys on the window ledge. Here lay her first error; in her haste to reach up through the broken window to get the keys and open the last remaining lock, she nicked her arm on the broken glass, causing it to bleed profusely, a heavy clue for a later pursuer. With all locks disarmed, she opened the kitchen door and made her way inside. Ah, no wonder it was so easy this time, she could tell by the change in decor, by the new brown kitchen carpet tiles and the general fresh smell that the house was now occupied by a new family. The constant robberies must have driven the last family out and in their haste to sell to the dewy-eyed love birds, whose dream house this obviously was, they neglected to mention the poor history the house held. As though the estate agents might advertise, 'A beautifully, detached three-bedroom house, in a quiet cul-de-sac, much sought after by burglars'. I don't think so!

Gold and currency. That was all she took, nothing more, nothing less. She prided herself on this. Drawers and cupboards were carefully checked. Her eyes danced around every crevice in the room, her fervour was almost palpable. She tensed her rectum as her churning stomach tried excitedly to push out last night's curry. She knew this feeling well and that it would ebb, as she became more familiar with her surroundings. A trickle of blood dropped from her arm, so she wrapped a kitchen towel around the wound and continued her search. She was a gentleman burglar, if there is such a thing, in that she left everything relatively tidy and never, like many burglars, emptied her bowels on the carpet and the furniture when the urge took her. She was familiar with the type of electric cooker in the kitchen, so quickly switched on the back ring to full, filled a saucepan of water and placed it on the ring to boil. Anyone who interrupted her at her work would have a new face, melted on with boiling water. She then nipped through the neatly furnished lounge across the brown soft-pile carpet to the front hall, pushing the latch down on the door lest anyone with a key should disturb her.

With her preparations complete, she made her way up the stairs to the bedrooms. This, usually, is where the booty lies. The two small bedrooms held nothing of interest for her. Now on to the master bedroom. She always liked to keep the best for last.

Passing the double divan to her left and the white fitted wardrobes to her right, she headed for the chest of drawers that held a red portable T.V. and two 'heaven-sent' jewellery boxes on top. Her pasty complexion elevated to pillar box red, in anticipation. She sat on the bed and opened them up to discover an Aladdin's cave of gold. Sovereign rings, chunky gold bracelets, three watches, ten gold chains, a solitary 24-carat gold sovereign coin, pendants and earrings. It was a jeweller's shop in a box.

She closed her eyes and shook her head as though to make sure it wasn't a mirage. Her January-dull face lit up like the fourth of July and, for a moment, a deep smile creased her face and she pocketed the gold in a small, velvet swag bag. Her hands shook so much that she thought she might drop it. She hurried down the stairs and out of the house, leaving the lock still on the front door, but turning off the electric cooker on her exit. She was away, and it was only one fifteen p.m.

On exiting the house she made her second, and by far her greatest mistake. It was my house she had just robbed.

Sharon, with her big eyes and pretty, inviting smile capped by sprightly and neat, short, gelled, dark hair, approached our house. The three p.m. bus from town dropped her right outside.

Her slight, curved frame, wasp waist and lady walk belied the ferocious fighting ability that her black belt stood as evidence.

When her key wouldn't turn in the lock she was baffled, but nothing more. 'Perhaps Geoff's in the garage and has locked the door for extra safety,' she thought as she wandered around the back. The kitchen window was broken and the door ajar.

Then she knew, but still tried to deny it to herself. 'Geoff's probably broken it by accident,' she lied to herself again. When she finally got to the bedroom to find a lifetime's worth of jewellery gone, there was no denying the obvious. We'd been robbed!

She sat on the bed not knowing what to do. Jewellery boxes were up-turned all over the bed. Tears welled and tried to explode in her eyes, but she held them back.

We'd only been in the house six weeks, nobody gets robbed after only six weeks, do they? She'd been so happy – overflowing with the stuff – now this, some bastard, some dirty bastard had been in her house, her bedroom, and rifled through her belongings.

She was veiled with an absolute feeling of helplessness. Her smarting eyes let out a single tear, she wished Geoff were home.

He'd know what to do.

My gold Sierra purred and shuddered to a halt outside the house. My heart rate increased at the sight of a police car occupying my parking space. I knew something was wrong, I just hoped it was nothing too serious. I racked my brain. When was the last time I gave someone a dig? Have they reported me?

Nothing came to mind, it had been weeks since I'd hit anyone and I was sure I'd taken that library book back. I hastily made my way into the house. There was muffled conversation coming from the kitchen. As I entered the lounge from the main door Sharon entered from the kitchen.

'We've been burgled.'

A feeling of great sadness ran through my body as I took her in my arms.

'Don't worry, I'll sort it out,' I told her as I sympathetically rubbed her back. She feigned a smile. My mind raced into overdrive, a thousand questions jamming the switchboard. The one most elevated and obvious being, 'Where the fuck do I start?' I went into the kitchen. Sharon's dad, a heavy-set, handsome man in his fifties was on his knees tacking a piece of hardboard over the broken window. A cocktail of feelings raced through me; hate, sadness, revenge and confusion all failing to find a loading place in my mind, nor an exit from my body. I wanted to make it all all right. Give Sharon an instant remedy.

But my miracle sack was as empty as a moron Christmas sack. I felt helpless and hurt, so resorted to the obvious.

'Some bastard's gonna pay for this!'

A fresh-faced policeman emerged from the hallway. Sympathetic, kind, and as helpless as us. He turned to Sharon whose eyes were beginning to smart again.

'Come down to the station love, when you feel a little better, and drop in a list of everything that's missing. Try not to touch anything until the fingerprints man has been.'

I picked up my black baseball bat from the brick fireplace, where it lay sentry for just such occasions. I held it firmly by handle and head, tapping out a bit of the aggression that was filling me fast.

My eyes glazed with hatred, the panda car pulled away from the outside of my house.

'Some bastard's gonna pay for this,' I said again, to no one in particular.

'You can't just go around hitting people,' Sharon blurted out rather uncharacteristically, popping the cork off her self-control.

'Don't fucking tell me what I can and can't do. As soon as I find out who's been in here I'm gonna fucking destroy them, and no cunt is going to stop me,' I shouted back. I said sorry straight away. I'd never even raised my voice to her before, nor her to me. She burst out of the room.

'I think she's a little upset Geoff,' interrupted the very observant Alan, Sharon's younger brother. I nodded a nod that was both apologetic and in agreement. They say you always hurt the ones you love. I quickly followed her up the stairs and gave her an apologetic hug. We were both fraught and anxious and it was already starting to take its toll. I was racking my brain for the solution. My head throbbed like a hammered thumb. Where to go, who to see, what to say, how to say it?

I hugged Sharon and felt her sadness. I picked up my bat and left the house on my 'hunt for gold'.

The bat was to be a visual tool. I find that people tend to listen to you more when you wield such an implement.

I knocked the door of a terraced, pre-war house that seemed acutely narrow. Dave, a tall, blond man in his late thirties answered. At the sight of my bat his eyes popped out of his head. He was a friend who was in the know. He invited me into the front room; unclean, though quite homely. His face froze in an uncomfortable smile. I told him my tale and asked for names. I wanted to know who the local thieves were and whom they dealt with. He'd lived here a long time and knew the local villains. Every area had one or two receivers, people who bought goods that were a little warm.

Longford's dealer, he informed me, was a man they called 'Duke'.

The name, the Duke, hinted at 'hard' – John Wayne and all that – but I didn't give a monkey's fuck. I wore my anger and ill-intent like a poster. I handed my karate business card, listing my qualifications in the world of combat and my phone number, to Dave.

'Tell anyone and everyone that I'm hunting for the person who had my stuff. When I find them I'm gonna break their fucking legs.' I lifted my bat to emphasise my intention. His pale complexion and frozen *Thunderbirds* smile told that my point was well made.

I was still seething with anger, not only had my possessions gone but my pride was severely dented.

I'm ashamed to say that I thought I was above being robbed. I hated myself for my own arrogance, for daring to feel superior, a trait I'd disliked in so many other people.

Smoothly over the narrow Black Horse Road bridge in my gold Sierra, I took a shady left into the road that housed the Duke.

The first door I knocked on was the wrong door, but the friendly recipient, whose eyes disappeared under a furrowed brow, pointed me in the right direction, despite the presence of my 'equaliser', the baseball bat.

'You're not going to hit him are you? He's my friend.'

'No, no,' I replied, 'we were just gonna have a game of baseball.'

What did he think I was going to do with it, pick my nose? I wondered what kind of friend it was that sent a man with a baseball bat to a said 'friend's' door. He was either stupid or a disgruntled neighbour pretending to be a mate.

Another door was knocked and another marble stare hit the bat I held so ominously. I told him my business and apologised for the unsolicited call. My invite into his warm and modestly clean, furnished front room, stretched not to my bat, so I left it at the front door of this terraced, quiet cul-de-sac pre-war house. I didn't need it really, my much-practised, often-used right hook seconded nicely if need be. His blonde, tall, attractive lady friend kindly offered me a cup of tea. I politely refused. The Duke eyed me with suspicion. I wouldn't have let me in. He was middle-aged with a crime-weathered face capped by light receding hair. He looked 'John Wayne rugged', which, I guess, had earned him the tab Duke. He tried to give me a hard look, and his effort wasn't bad, but I'd seen hard, and this wasn't it, though the mask would fool most. Again, I told my tale and proffered my business card and 'I'm gonna break legs' warning that was to become the epistle of this saga. He looked at my business card for a few seconds. He pondered on it, then his eyes lit up and he pointed to me, dropping the hard mask that hadn't fooled me anyway.

'Ah, you're Geoff Thompson.'

I admired his perception.

'Wasn't it you that had your cheque stolen last year and hunted it down?' (Story in *Watch My Back*.)

I smiled. I was flattered that my escapade had reached the ears of people right in Coventry's deepest corners.

'Yeah, that's right. That was a long time ago.'

'You're not having much luck, are you?'

I shook my head. We talked a little more and he gave me another contact and his assurance that should my gold fall on his doorstep he'd redirect it back to me.

The contact he gave me was Frank, the second-hand dealer. Frank was a friend of mine from the stolen cheque saga so was on my list anyway. On the way to Frank's lay the Saracen's Head, the Coach and Horses, the Billiard Hall, the Griffen and Carney's, all Longford drinking holes.

Within half an hour I'd visited them all, left my card, my tale of woe and intentions to landlords/ladies and punters. My purpose here was twofold. I was not so naïve as to believe that they'd ring me up if they'd heard tell of my estranged loot, though even an off-chance was worth a shot. Rather I wanted everyone in the district to know that my house had been robbed. I wanted it to be a common talking point in the Locals so that eventually the news of my hunt would fall on the ears of the guilty party and that I wasn't a man to take it lying down. It wasn't just my gold at stake, or my pride; the security of my new house was in question. It was important to me that every crook around knew what to expect if they fucked with me. There was no burglar alarm better than that of fear – or a belt round the face with a bat – and if I had to hurt someone to get the point across, then so be it. Most of these thieves were languid bastards anyway, so it wouldn't take a lot of doing.

I arrived at Frank-the-dealer's abode. Apparently news travels faster than a Sierra two-litre, and news of my hunt had already reached him when I entered the cosy front room of his terraced Longford Road house. The Duke was sat with Frank and a cup of tea. The room was nice. It was a year since I'd last visited Frank, hunting for my stolen dole cheque. The room was plain, and though clean, in need of a face-lift. Now it sported an expensive leather chesterfield, sat neatly on deep-piled Axminster and a fireplace built from hand-made brick that chimneyed to the ceiling. Fate had obviously blown some nice gear into his second-hand business. Frank smiled, showing a gap where his front teeth used to reside. His dark skin was warmly creased around the eyes, his long, apache, black hair lay shining and flat, cascading down to his shoulders. Frank ran a local second-hand shop. He was a real character who knew everyone worth knowing. As I entered the front room the Duke rose and greeted me like an old friend. By his darting look to my right side, I could tell that he liked me all the better without my bat. Debbie, Frank's attractive wife smiled shyly up from the chesterfield. I sensed that she liked me and was at home with people of my ilk; her brother and late father had been of a similar gait.

After the usual pleasantries we got down to business. Who'd been in my house? Frank dealt with all the thieves and if he didn't know, no one would.

'How did they gain entry to the house?' Frank asked.

I wondered what difference it made. Apparently, it made a lot.

'Through the back door.'

'How?'

Another stupid question, but he was the boss.

'By smashing the window.'

'And what was taken?'

'Gold.'

'Nothing else. Just gold?'

'Yeah, I've got loads of stuff in the house as well, but nothing else was touched.'

Frank looked across at Debbie knowingly. She smiled.

'Sounds like M,' he said with an ever-so-slight hint of reluctance and a slight whistle as the words left the gap between his teeth. 'She breaks glass and she takes gold. There's a couple at it, but this is her gaff. I'd be very surprised if it's not her. She used to slaughter all her gear to me, but we had words about a year ago, and she deals somewhere else now.' He thought for a moment, then looked at Debbie again.

'You know her Deb, dark-haired bird, with the big sewer mouth.' He shot a glance to me. 'Horrible piece she is, evil mouth on it. Just got married to Scotch P from Woodend.'

Debbie nodded her agreement.

'Right dirty slag,' she concluded. She was very descriptive.

So, I was looking for a 'right dirty slag called M with an evil mouth on it'. Knowing the areas that I was about to go into, that didn't help too much, most of them could major in 'mouthy slag'; probably even a few potential Ph.D.s there too.

When the conversation reached an *impasse*, I thanked them cordially for their help and left with the name inscribed on my brain and a piece of cigarette paper with my next contact on; Fency, so called because he fenced anything from cheap ladies' underwear to Armani suits, from job lots of kids' sweets to hard drugs. If crime pays, his cheque must have still been in the post because the street in Foleshill where he lived looked like a bombsite in Beirut. It never ceased to amaze me that these so-called crooks and drug dealers who purported to earn 'good money' nearly always lived in the pits of deprivation. Either the 'good money' was squandered or it simply wasn't 'good money'. People are always saying, 'Hey, John earns some coin on those drugs.'

Oh really, is that why he's still living in a shit-hole in Woodend? Fuck off!

I stood outside Fency's house and knocked on the paint-flaking door, but it worried me. A lad could catch a nasty disease off a door that dirty. The four square glass windows it held were filmed with dirt. As the door opened the smell of take-away food, dogs and dodgy central heating hit me like a blow to the stomach. A churlish, marble stare challenged me. Fency, unlike Duke, needed no mask for unwelcome strangers. He was a scary fucker. Hard, shorter than myself at five foot ten, with mousy, light hair and a 'Mars Bar' as thick as a pencil running right across his nose. He chewed his dinner and stared up at me. His teeth were the colour of a banana and his face had a permanent grimace.

'Yeah?' he said without interrupting his chewing.

'Frank-the-dealer sent me.'

He looked behind me, then to my left and right. He had that kind of 'who-the-fuck-are-you' look on his face. I felt about as welcome as a dose.

'You'd better come in.'

If I thought the street was scruffy then I was in for a surprise when I saw his front room. Old chip papers, empty and half-empty crisp packets, magazines and newspapers all looked at home littered on and around the furniture. An old tinfoil Chinese take-away tray lay forlorn under the television, with dried and hardened sauce stains on its base. Poor bastard, we've got a video under our telly.

This was a scruffy front room. Everyone has the right to be dirty, but this man was abusing the privilege. To match the war-torn living space, I expected his woman to be an Amazonian-type girl with childbearing hips, and a Henry Cooper left hook. I was surprised to be confronted by a coffee-proffering lady with a sweet voice and disposition. I declined the kind offer of coffee.

I introduced myself and told of my business, but Fency still seemed a little unapproachable. Understandable, I guess, as I was a stranger asking unsolicited questions.

His eyes seemed in a permanent state of squint, and he was still chewing, yet there didn't seem to be any food in his mouth.

'You came highly recommended,' I said, trying to sweeten him up a little, and loosen his tongue.

This seemed to do the trick. Over the next fifteen minutes he spilled all his contacts, dealings and general theories on the histrionics of crime and its workings. The name M and 'right mouthy slut' were mentioned again.

Eventually I managed to get out of the house without catching anything. Another handshake saw me back on the road, head still pounding, and my violent alter-ego dying to burst forth and teach someone a lesson. I'd got a name, so it was a start.

Many, many more houses and public houses were visited, and then the next day I'd visit all of the second-hand shops.

'You'll never find out who's done it Geoff,' said my friend smartly as we stood talking on the Devon door.

'I fucking will,' I snapped back. I was still a little tense.

'D'ya reckon?'

'I don't reckon nothin'. I *know*. I might not get my gold back, but I'm gonna dish out some pain when I find out who's had it.'

My companion's mouth curved into a smirk. Apparently he didn't think so.

Another fucking sleepless night, tossing and turning. Me and Sharon had to sleep on a mattress on the floor of the spare room, so as not to disturb vital police evidence.

'Try not to touch anything until the fingerprints man has been,' we were told by the ever-so-sympathetic copper who'd seen and done it all before.

Nothing in life was about to shock this man. Burglaries were way down at the bottom of his shopping list of stress/shock-related incidents. He'd once had to bag up the cadaver of an unfortunate born-again Christian whose skull was split wide and gaped, issuing blood and brain. The guy's lung lay by his side on the floor where the home-made killing implement – something akin to a sickle – had left it after dragging it from his chest. The attacker, a devil-worshipping brain-dead, had taken offence at the Christian's preaching. No. burglaries were definitely mundane by comparison.

Again, I was in the company of stress-related insomnia. Sharon was there too. All night I could feel her sadness. It was almost tangible. I pulled her close to me and kissed her gently on the lips, hoping to ease her pain, at the same time knowing nothing could. The damage was done, though I've got to say she did bear the sadness stoically.

You don't realise how many second-hand shops there are in one city until you've cause to visit them. There's fucking loads. The next morning I made it my business to visit them all in the hope that I could block off all the lines of exit that my gold might take. I knew it would be offered around one of these places, so I had to let the shop owners know that if they brought it, I'd be after them too. I was neither rude nor impolite, I just planted the seed. It worked too, because one of my friends in the trade said that all the dealers were ringing each other up:

'Who's this mad bastard, Geoff Thompson? Have you had his gear?'

'No.'

'Well don't take it. He's a fucking nut case.'

Etc, etc, etc.

I didn't need to tell the dealers that I was going to break their legs, the implication would be enough.

'You tell them,' I'd say, wagging a condemning finger, 'that I'm on their trail, and when I find them, which I will, I'm gonna break their fucking legs.'

The added expletive helped to underline my intent. If you want to get through to these fuckers you have to be able to talk their language. Sometimes the parlance needs to be physical.

The man in front of me, over twenty stone and as cool as a December pudlock, was 'the man' in this city. And a big man he was too. His head looked like a pea on a mountain, he was the biggest thing I'd ever seen without an engine. Everything about him was authoritative. He was also my close friend. On hearing of my loss he made a few discreet inquiries. When I visited him at his abode I was pleased to hear the name M for the third time, but it wasn't until I visited a pub in Bell Green that I had absolute confirmation.

'Whoever it is that's had my gold,' I told the heavy-set landlord, 'cut their arm on my glass door as they went in.'

His eyes lit up and he ushered me across to one side. He lifted thumb and forefinger to chin and thought deeply before speaking. The balcony that hung above his belt expanded almost to bursting point as he sighed, and I thought it might push me out of the room. He had to be careful about what he said; he didn't want to be thought of as a grass; comebacks from the people in question would be heavy if they knew it was him who'd told.

'There was a girl in here yesterday at about one thirty p.m. with a cut on her arm.'

'Was her name M by any chance?' I asked.

'Yeah, that's right. Married to Scotch P.'

YI AHH! I'd got her. I'd fucking *got* her.

'Be careful, though Geoff,' he continued, 'P's' a nasty piece of work, good with a blade.'

'We'll see,' I said, as my heart raced with a cocktail of fear, excitement and exhilaration.

I opened my front door and walked deftly across the brown-carpeted front hall to the living room. Sharon was busy ironing.

'I've got her, I've fucking got her,' I told her excitedly, then regaled her with the details.

Sharon was equally excited. We shared a hug. Her supple body fitted against mine like a glove – but that's another story entirely. We both felt elated because we knew that this thing was nearly over, all I had to do now was set the scene.

'I want to come with you when you get her,' Sharon said.

'No! Thanks, but no. I'll do it. I know you want to go and I admire your bottle, but I have to do it on my own.'

She did have the bottle but, I don't know, I just didn't feel it was right for her to come with me.

Anyway, now I had a definite name, I was on my way. A quick coffee and I was off again.

I visited the Bell Green club, Bell Inn, Rose and Crown, Green Man, Golden Fleece and one or two more pubs in the next hour. This time though, I was hunting for a specific name: Scotch P. I knew he drank in all of these places, specifically the Bell Green club. I would confront him and demand what was mine. If he so much as breathed out of place, I would destroy him on the spot. If he wanted to 'go', he'd better be fucking good with that knife. Every pub that I entered that afternoon, I prepared myself to fight him and anyone with him. That's the only way that you can cope with this type of situation, imagine the worst case scenario, then tell yourself that 'you can handle it'. Every pub I entered that afternoon hadn't seen P today. I handed each pub a card and said:

'Tell P I'm looking for him.'

I walked into the Bell Green, a typical working men's club with a large bar and a scattering of cheap tables and chairs. I approached the bar to be greeted by a young girl with more make-up than face, and more tits than dress. She had a kind smile, the kind that scared the shit out of me. You'd need a police escort just to sleep with her, you know the type.

'I'm looking for Scotch P, is he in?' I scanned the bar as I spoke.

'That's 'is family over there,' she said and nodded her head at a rough group of people sat at the back of the bar room.

I approached the table that sat about eight of the roughest-looking specimens this side of the ugly farm. A native family from the Gourbels that could Ugly for

Scotland. It took me a few seconds to fathom the men from the women. They were playing cards. None looked up as I approached. That was the game. It's meant to imply that you're 'not a threat' in fact so little of a threat that they're not even going to look up. I knew the game. I liked it. I'd played it many times before, but with better players than these. I counter-attacked by drilling a stare into them one by one. In this arena a stare is a subliminal 'challenge-to-fight'. My stare said just that: 'I'm ready to fight you all'. My counter was acknowledged by a nod from one of the men. The nod looks like a friendly gesture, really it's a bottle-drop. My heart began to race.

'Where's P?' I asked, hiding the quiver in my voice. His brother, long hair, face like Shergar, threw me the kind of cold look that was supposed to say 'don't fuck' but just read 'scared'. I knew he was shitting himself, if he wasn't we'd have been fighting already. I threw a look back that said 'don't give a fuck'. I think he got it because his eyes hit the floor like marbles. The rest of the family carried on as though I wasn't there, feigning disconcern. I knew that they were concerned and that the very act of me entering their lair alone had unnerved them. It hinted at psychotic. I knew it would. Sun Tzu said, twenty-five centuries ago (he never actually said it to me personally); 'if you know your enemy and know yourself, you need not fear the result of a hundred battles.' I did know my enemy, and I definitely knew myself. He also said that the supreme act of war was to subdue the enemy without fighting. This was also big in my game plan. By the time I actually found P, a dozen of his friends and family would have already told him that I was looking for him. He'll have put the feelers out to see who I am and what kind of fire-power I hold. The feed-back will have scared him shitless. If my ploy worked that is, if not we'd be fighting and I was already well prepared for that.

'He's nort hearr!' came the thick Glaswegian reply.

Casually I skimmed my business card across the card table like a cool thing, and fixed his gaze until he turned away.

'Tell 'im Geoff Thompson's looking for 'im. He ought t' ring.'

At that, I smiled, turned, and walked out of the club. As I left I could feel the hairs (what few I have left) on the back of my neck rise in anticipation of a 'Judas' attack. It never came. I was pleased.

Wednesday, five p.m. I arrived back home from an afternoon's bricklaying, done mostly in auto-mode. My mind was far away from bricks and mortar, an eternity from spirit-level and jointing-iron. I was oblivious to the deep ache in my lower back. My mind was obsessed with revenge, turmoiled by violent thoughts and geared up totally to the recovery of my stolen gold. I was beginning to feel a little weak. Stress of this intensity takes its toll and can weaken you immeasurably. The real fight isn't in the pubs/clubs, it's with yourself, every minute of the day, a continual battle in your own head.

Sharon's pretty face cheered me up, as it always did. Her big, bright, sea green eyes sparkled a welcome that I'd come to love. I kissed her and took her in my arms holding her tightly and, savouring the perfumed smell from her soft neck, I kissed her gently on the lips.

'You've had three calls from a Scottish chap,' she said. 'I told him you'd be back at five thirty p.m.'

'How did he sound?' I asked, looking for clues as to how he was handling it.

'He sounded a little worried,' she smiled back.

'Good, that's exactly how I want him.'

I relaxed in a chair and sipped a hot coffee. I usually really enjoy a relax and a drink, but in times of stress nothing is fully enjoyed.

The 'tring' of the telephone broke my daydream and made me jump. Sharon came from out of the kitchen to spectate. I slowly ambled over to the phone, but didn't pick it up straight away. Let the fucker sweat, the extra few rings would kill him.

'Hello,' I said, eventually lifting the receiver, my stomach clenching in apprehension.

'Geoff,' came the soft Scottish voice on the other end of the line, 'this is P. I hear you've been looking for me.' Without waiting for my answer he continued, 'somebody sayd you think ma messus has rorbed yuar husse. A've had a werrd wiy' 'er and she seys she knows nethin' aboot it.'

I'd expected him to deny it initially, but it still disappointed me when he did. I'd hoped it might be easier.

'P, you know, an' I know, that she's 'ad my gold. So, don't play games wi' me, y' know 'oo I am and what I'll do. I'm trying to be nice about this s' don't take the piss. I'm a fair man and I'm givin' you one chance. Get m' gold back and that'll be the end of it, if not, you're gonna 'ave big problems, I don't wan' 'oo 'ave t' come t' your 'ouse.'

'Ded you come to my husse las' neight?' he asked.

'No, not las' night,' I replied, suppressing a smile. Someone had obviously knocked on his door the night before and because he thought it was me he'd not answered. I had visions of him and M hiding behind the settee holding the dog's mouth shut in case he barked and gave them away.

'I'll give you a week to get it back,' I concluded.

'OK,' he said quietly.

I put the phone down.

In that moment of negotiation, a week had seemed a reasonably short time to wait. By Friday my head was shot to pieces with the thought of having to wait another five days, and I was beginning to regret giving him such a long time. I should have demanded it there and then. Every day I waited I got more frustrated and angry. I wanted to go to his house and drag him and her out and demand what was mine. I wondered if I could realistically expect ever to see my gold again. Did he agree to get it back only in the hope that after a week or so I'd let it drop? Perhaps he'd find a sudden surge of bravery and defy me to get it back off him, perhaps using the seven days to gather an army. I decided to give him the week, as I'd agreed, then if it were fruitless, I'd visit his house at four a.m. in the morning and pebble-dash the house and him. I'd batter the pair of them in their bed. To give myself some time, I'd ring the Bell Green police station with a red herring on the other side of the district to give me 'in-and-out' time.

P's second-floor flat lay on the edge of the roughest part of Woodend, in Pailton Close, recently the scene of mass battles between locals and the police. There were more broken noses here than at a boxers' convention. I watched the news the night before, it said 'Twenty dead in Sarajevo' – that's just a stag night in Woodend. His flat backed on to a field and an industrial estate that lay deserted by night. I parked my car on the narrow road at the beginning of the estate, just a couple of hundred yards from the flats. I tucked a Samurai sword under my long coat and walked slowly down the grass hill and across a little field to Pailton Close. The moonless, early evening sky reduced me to just a shadow. The smell of burning rubbish in the distance wafted into my nose. These Woodend hovels were like army barracks.

Burnt-out cars lay abandoned on the edge of the estate; playgrounds for latchkey kids. Dull lights emitted from behind the yellowed net curtains, which were stuck to condensation-soaked windows, that is, the ones without boards on them. Many of the people occupying these kennels were in worse repair than the flats, so I guess it worked well.

Between the blocks of flats was a concrete maze of walls and paths and entryways. It looked as though it was designed by a mugger. It was important that I targeted P's flat, so that if needs be I could be in, do the dirty deed, and be out again quickly.

It was said that there were so many burglaries in this area that you daren't close the window at night for fear of trapping someone's fingers.

When I finally did find my number it took all my will power not to go, there and then, and knock down the door, demand my gold, beat the shit out of them both and be away. No! I disciplined myself. I'd made a deal and that was it, no door-knocking until the week was up. I also knew that my temper was growing to a ten on the Richter scale and knocking his door might just shoot it off the page completely, then I'd be looking at a charge of aggravated burglary carrying a possible seven years in prison. The courts don't look kindly on vigilantes. Could I actually go to prison for retrieving my own gold from a thief?

Reluctantly, I jogged back to my car, timing myself. Thirty seconds. Probably two minutes to get into his flat, do the job and get out, thirty seconds back to the car, and another minute for miscellaneous. That's four minutes in all. I wondered if P and M knew just how close they'd come.

I drove away satisfied in the knowledge that I had set the scene, just in case.

I'd been intending to insure the contents of the house ever since I moved in, but never actually got around to it, as is always the way. A quick phone call to 'Sheffield' Johnny sorted that little problem. A bit of post-dated insurance was assured. June, he told me, worked for an insurance company and was crazy about him; she'd sort it out.

John was a very charismatic man with a thirst for crime and a hunger for violence. He was also hugely funny with an uncannily accurate philosophy on life. He sported long silver-white hair and a beard to match, and a heavy scar (picked up in a bar in Glasgow) split the right side of the beard neatly in two. He wore the scar proudly, the scar gave him character; it was a badge of battle. His whole body was a canvass of indian ink tattoo.

'Get yer sen a dorg,' he told me in that deep, Scottish accent.

'Bearter than any alarm, an' all is bull-shit aboot having to take them for a walk every day, don't listen to it son.

I've had dorgs for twenty years and never took them for a walk yet.'

The police fingerprints man knocked on my front door. It was late afternoon, almost the end of the working day. Ours was just one of many houses he'd been to that week, ten that day. I invited him in. He was a weather-beaten, handsome type of man, in an ill-fitting grey suit, and an equally grey white shirt with its top button unfastened and tie loosened in a kind of bedraggled way. His black leather shoes looked like they'd done a dozen marathons.

The irony of policing is that, even before they visit a burgled house they've got a pretty good idea who's done the job, but they can't arrest them without absolute evidence. The way the law stands they've practically got to catch them in the act *and* get a full confession.

In the nineties, the job of the policeman is like playing a game of football against a team with movable goal posts, a blind referee and a team captain who's not on your side.

Coffee and biscuits were proffered, and he eagerly accepted, the poor man looked like he hadn't eaten in ages. The trouble was, people who've been robbed never seem to be in the mood to offer refreshments, mostly they are crest-fallen and un-talkative, the last thing you want to do is ask someone who's just had their life's belongings stolen for coffee and biscuits.

'Look,' he told us straight, through a biscuit-filled mouth, 'the chances of ever seeing your gold again, or in fact of catching the people responsible for taking it are negligible. You've got more chance of winning the pools. I've visited forty houses this week, and believe me, you've been lucky, some of the victims have had the whole house emptied, and everything they own gone in an instant. Some of them are old people who have not only lost their belongings, they've also lost their peace of mind, many never recover. You're both young and strong, you'll get over it, but they probably never will.'

All this did was harden my resolve to 'do it myself'.

To say I was pissed off with waiting was an understatement, and by Monday I was pacing the room. I decided to pay my friend a visit.

The Rose and Crown lay, daringly, just off the Bell Green Road, one level high, with lounge and bar entrances to the left and right respectively. Not unattractive as pubs go, though sparse inside with a scattering of tables and chairs and a run of soft seating by the bar's bay-window that sat the old, the drunk and the infirm. To the right of the entrance, just inside the bar sat the six, all uniform in their hard and scarred faces.

In my bright red and green Nike tracksuit, Fila boots and leather Fila cap, I strolled in, my confident gait hiding my churning stomach. Straight to the bar. The barman's eyes darted from me to the group in the corner.

'That them?' I said evenly without turning my head to look.

He nodded. There were a few other people sat around the bar who watched with interest as I approached the table.

Up until now I had never met P and had only had vague descriptions given to me; 'wanker', 'arse-hole' that kind of thing. But that didn't help, I mean, everyone fitted that description. I'd have to bash half of Woodend. On arriving at the table I didn't know which one was P. Nobody looked up, maybe hoping that I'd just disappear. The landlord looked over from the bar anxiously, he didn't want trouble in his pub. There was an palpable tension in the air.

I approached the Addams family. To my right was a heavy-set man in his early twenties, with a face like a burglar's dog and a nasty run of spots across his chin that could have come with free garlic bread. He had a bulbous nose that had 'target' written all over it. Next to him, P's brother, whom I'd already met in the Bell Green club. He looked down at the table to avoid my glare. Then a man with a pencil-neck and a tight, small face (mostly hidden by his over-sized baseball cap), the horrendous scar that ran down his right cheek as wide as the blade that put it there. He was as ugly as a troll's woman. An older man next to him, with dark, cropped hair, an involuntary smile and darting eyes that wanted to meet mine but dare not.

The air was thick with smoke and tension as I walked across wearing my hardest face and employing a walk that said to anyone who knew 'walks': 'don't fuck with me today'. I stopped at the table, opened my eyes wide and grimaced. The adrenaline was racing around like a trapped bluebottle. I used the 'duck syndrome' to hide my fear; calm above the waters, legs going like fuck underneath. I was here now, and I was ready to do it. They were all sitting down, so I had an edge. I stood back slightly from the table so that I could kick the head off the closest to me if any of them ran at the lip. Then I'd get into the rest before they had a chance to react. Hopefully the first two or three would be picking up teeth before the others knew what was happening. I remembered the words of the legendary Japanese sword master Musashi; 'when dealing with multiple opponents you must attack first and keep attacking until the danger subdues.' That sounded good to me.

My ploy was to ask for P by name. If the reply were hostile in any way, shape or form I'd go into 'psycho-mode' and attack everything that moved, straight away. I didn't really expect to win against six opponents, but I felt sure that I could remove a nose and a couple of ears before they got the better of me. I'd definitely leave my mark. Do I sound brave? I didn't feel brave; I was shitting myself. This may sound barbaric, but that's what you need when you're dealing with 'barbarians', after all you can't be a pussycat if you're fighting a tiger. Somebody that you've 'marked' also serves as a lifetime's walking billboard advertising *you* as a man 'not to fuck with'. No one fixed my gaze. Yes, I liked this; this was a good sign.

'P,' I said with a hint of authoritative malice.

I was shocked at their response. I was expecting some kind of animosity, but got none. Instead they universally pointed to P, even his brother sat there pointing a condemning finger. So much for family loyalty. P's head shot around to catch a glimpse of me; our eyes met. A deep scar underlined his cheek bone, a scruffy uncut beard covered most of his whey face, all topped by the customary canvas baseball cap sported by most of Coventry's criminal youth. Bits of his thinning hair pushed out from the sides of the hat like straw. He may have looked like a scarecrow but he wasn't doing much scaring today. His shoulders and back hunched forward and I had the sudden urge to kick him clean out of the chair. I resisted.

'OUTSIDE!' I ordered. He jumped out of the chair and followed me. I lined him up as a matter of course.

The busy Bell Green traffic hummed in the background. Shoppers walked past oblivious to what was occurring. Someone getting a 'dig' in this district was not unusual. P fidgeted. He kept his hands in his blue stained tracksuit, pockets which told me that he didn't want to fight. I let my hands hang loosely by my sides, telling him that I did. I stared at his weasel face and wondered whether I shouldn't bash him where he stood. Crush him flatter than a shadow. His chin looked temptingly close and mighty suspect. I couldn't do it. I'd given my word that if he delivered the goods that would be the end of it. My word meant a lot to me. I also felt a little sorry for him, though I shouldn't have, he'd stabbed many before me and lived a life of crime. Violence was his way. The fact that he looked scared meant nothing, a frightened man if pushed too far is a dangerous man capable of dangerous acts. The key to keeping someone frightened is to make them feel that there is a way out, give them a little hope. If they feel that there is no hope then- they become desperate, employing desperate measures. Many a good man has been defeated chasing a 'beaten' man. Some of my friends had said, 'give it 'im anyway', but I couldn't go back on my word. Even in this volatile environment you are only as good as your word.

I checked the pub door to make sure that his companions hadn't followed. They hadn't, we were alone.

'Where's my gear, man?'

'I've got it Geoff, I've got it,' he spluttered. He must have felt sure that he was about to get a dig. 'I've rung you three times today already. I'll bring it to the Bell Green club tonight.'

I eyed him suspiciously, had he really got it, or was he just trying to save himself a hiding and buy a little time?

'You've definitely got it?'

'Yeah, yeah. I'll bring it to the Bell Green club tonight, seven thirty.'

'Don't let me down P,' I said evenly, hiding my inner elation.

Then, as an afterthought:

'No, don't meet me at the club, you know where your flat is?'

He nodded hesitantly, of course he knew where it was.

'Meet me on the field at the back of your block of flats.'

His eyes shot forward like a cartoon cat trapped by the neck in a window. My ploy had the desired effect. His mouth fell open like a cash register, 'I knew you'd find out where I lived, I knew it', I could see him thinking.

I knew he'd react like that when I told him I knew where he lived.

'And another thing, P, tell M that my street is out of bounds from now on, tell her to keep away.'

'I will,' and then, 'I gave her a slap for ye, Geoff, t' teach her a lesson.' He was trying to buy my favour. It wasn't for sale.

At this I left, happy in the knowledge that I was nearly there, though I was still not sure I could believe him. I hoped, for his sake, that he wasn't lying.

My plan now was to meet P that evening on the green at the back of his flat in Pailton Close, get out of my car as he approached, accompanied by my four foot long

Samurai sword. I wouldn't hit him or even threaten him with it. I'd stick it in the grass next to my feet. That'd be enough.

P obviously thought my reasons for the secluded meeting was so that I could retrieve my gold and give him a thorough thraping. Just as I knew his idea of meeting at the much-populated Bell Green club was to ensure that I didn't give him the said thraping. After all, just by the nature of it, pain was uncomfortable and best avoided. He'd had a bit of it in his time judging by his face and wasn't about to court any more, thank you very much. What P didn't realise was that I was a man of my word. Another thing he obviously didn't realise was, that if I did want to 'cane' him, a few witnesses wouldn't stop me from doing so. I'm stupid like that, if I decide to hit someone, I don't care if the Chief of Police is watching, they're gonna have it.

At the thought of the aforementioned 'pain', he got his sister to ring me up at five p.m. and say that he'd been arrested and that she would come in place of him with my gold. A cop-out, I know, but who gives a fuck, as long as I get back what's mine I'm not bothered who hands it over.

At seven fifteen p.m. Sharon kissed me good-bye, a worried look in her eyes belying her stoical front. And what a nice front it was too. She handed me my sword, bat, and steel fist. She's a good girl. I felt a little like a factory worker going to do a shift, but instead of my lady handing me a flask and sandwiches she hands me my fighting implements. I probably wouldn't use them but I'd take them just in case it was a set-up and I arrived to find a team waiting in the shadows of Bell Green for me.

Goodness knows I'd made enough enemies there over the years. My friend Alan had advised against the sword.

'If there *is* a team waiting for you, you'll use it and half of Bell Green will be walking around with limbs missing,' he'd pointed out.

The thing is though, if they did set me up, it would be what they deserved. Al had also offered to go with me as had John 'Awesome' Anderson and many others, but the way I saw it, it had to be done on my own.

I arrived at the Bell Green club car park five minutes early. Big mistake! Five minutes may not seem long, but in times of stress, facing possible violence and with time distortion twisting a knife, it's a fucking eternity. Your arse-hole becomes a manhole.

To the left of me was the back entrance to the shops. To my right, down about four steps, the Bell Green working men's club. Directly in front of me high communal garages that ran the entire length of the 200 foot car park. Behind me a long, high run of privet hedge, that looked precariously out of place in this concrete farm. There was only one entrance to this 'mugger friendly' car park and two exits – the second via ambulance.

Every car that entered the dark car park looked ominous, every group of people approaching like the enemy. I felt like leaving and going home. There was a desperate loneliness enveloping me and I wondered what the fuck I was doing here when I could be at home with my lady. I wanted to be anywhere but here. These seconds before battle scared me most, weakened me immeasurably, and made me sad and lonely beyond comprehension. Everything inside me said, 'RUN, RUN, RUN', only the captaining granite of self-control held me together. These seconds before battle are the hardest, harder than the fighting, harder than the training – those are just physical, quite easy by comparison. Adversity has an uncanny way of putting your life into perspective. It makes you appreciate the finer things in life, like a walk in the park, a cup of tea by the fire, lying in a warm bed with a loving mate listening to an orchestra of rain playing a symphony on the window. All of the things whose beauty lies hidden behind the curtain of familiarity re-expose themselves and spring to life as you see them being taken away from you.

All the time that these feelings were burgeoning I kept a hard, even look on my face as though nothing frightened me.

A group of heavy-set lads who looked like they'd come straight off the *Flintstones* set walked from out of the precinct towards my car. I scanned the faces for familiarity. I saw none. As they got closer, one looked as though he was carrying some kind of bat or shotgun. In the dark and from a distance I couldn't be sure. They got closer. Was it them? Was it a set-up? I gripped the corded handle of my sword and readied myself. The adrenaline reached fever pitch. They were almost on top of me. Should I start the car and drive off? There were four of them, all ugly as fuck; should I drive the car into them? I gripped the inside handle of my Sierra ready to open it and fight. I let the adrenaline loose slightly to give myself a little anger. When they came for me I'd let the lot out.

This is where it's really at; the single moment before a fight breaks many men. You have to run with it, accept it, be one with it, welcome it, bathe in the anguish, and even invite it in greater proportions. That's the way to beat it, but it's fucking hard. They walked past my car and down the steps into the club. I breathed a sigh of relief.

A girl approached my car. She was small and pretty, with long dark hair and a cute body. Her black trousers blew in the cool evening breeze. She pulled a worn mid-length sheepskin close to her body as protection against the weather. An older woman in a heavy butterfly-collared coat and a heavily flowered hat followed her. She looked like a musketeer. Up close I noticed that she sported a broken nose. It looked precariously out of place on what was otherwise a gentle, elderly lady. Broken faces are a common feature on women married into 'crime families'. It's kind of sad because underneath you can usually see a lovely girl or woman just praying to get out. In these kinds of environments the men keep the women in place with a hand of iron. One or two that I know personally have been literally crippled for daring to 'forget their place'.

I got out of my car to greet them. Looking all around for the possible set-up. Even my car was parked for a quick getaway.

'Geoff,' said the sweet, Scottish voice, 'P was arrested at the pub this morning, so I've come in his place.' We shook hands.

'Come and sit in the car,' I was trying to be as nice as possible, I have a lot of respect for ladies and after all, my argument was not with them. I opened the front passenger door for the younger of the two. My sword was sat on the front seat. I wanted her to see it.

'You should have seen the size of the sword he had with him, P,' I knew she would say when she reported back to him.

'Thank fuck I didn't go,' he'd reply.

D'artagnon opened the back door of the car and climbed in. The young woman climbed in the front. 'AHH!' she shouted involuntarily. She nearly died of shock at the sight of the sword.

'Sorry about that,' I said moving it to make room for her.

The young girl introduced the musketeer in the back seat as her mother – P's' mother. Fucking hell, I was gobsmacked. The man had sent his mum.

'P couldn't come,' she told me from the back seat.

'He got arrested at the dole this afternoon.'

My eyes met with the young girl in the front. She'd said on the phone that he was arrested in the pub this morning, and the mother had just said he was arrested in the dole this afternoon. Basically, this meant that he hadn't been arrested at all. He was probably under the table at home searching for his bottle. I never mentioned it. Things were embarrassing enough already.

'My P doesn't go into houses. It's that slag M that he married. My boys don't do that, they only rob shops,' the mother continued.

'I steal from shops,' the sister said frankly, 'but I never go into houses.' Her pride was obvious though possibly a little displaced. The sister handed me a small, black velvet purse. I leaned over and kissed her on the cheek.

I opened up the bag to reveal what I never really expected to see again; my gold. I couldn't suppress a smile.

'P's' a bit worried,' said the sister, beginning the bargain that I knew was inevitable.

'Tell him not to worry. I'm a man of my word. As far as I'm concerned, this,' I lifted up my bag of gold, 'is the end of it. If I see P in the street, I'll bear no grudges. But tell M to keep out of my street. If I see her there again, I'm gonna set my girlfriend on her; she's a black belt and is dying to get into her.' They both gasped at the words 'black belt'. I thought they might.

If I said Sharon was pleased when I returned with the loot, it would be an understatement. She dived on me and told me I was her hero. I knew that.

The threat of violence in this case was employed, the use of it thankfully was not. I see myself as a loaded gun; sometimes you can get the desired effect by just pointing it in the right direction.

Back home, loot in hand and trouble over, peace was restored and the aftermath began. It hit me like an axe. Aftermath comes after adversity. After you have taken your body and mind to their physical and mental limits you often experience a temporary emotional attack. If you've been exposed to big build-ups of adrenaline and it isn't released in fight or flight, as was the case this time, the aftermath is worse. Usually I prepare myself for the aftermath just by expecting it because when you expect something to hit you the impetus is lessened. This time, due to the elation of having retrieved my gold without even having to fight, I forgot my preparation.

Sharon had gone to visit her Nan. I was alone in the house when it started: the depression, the shame, the hate, the worry. I felt like I was dying inside. Then the tears, gushing out like floods. Then the shame for crying. I sat in a chair wanting to disappear into its arms. I was beyond comforting. I jumped out of the chair screaming and punched the wall several times until my hands swelled and bled. Then I felt ashamed for damaging myself and cried again.

3. Face to Face with Death

There are not many doormen who do not, at one time or another, worry about killing someone. Some worry a little, others a lot. I fall into the last category. I think and worry about it constantly. A doorman killed one of my old school friends in his tender twenties, and just lately, every time you open a newspaper you read about a doorman having killed somebody. In my time I have knocked over fifty opponents unconscious whilst 'on duty'. Every single time I worried myself sick until they 'came around', and even then worried for a couple of days in case they relapsed into a coma which, it seems, can be quite a common occurrence these days.

Every time I watch a T.V. programme or film glorifying violence, I think about that overwhelming feeling of fear I get every time I knock somebody out, their pale, chalky, lifeless faces failing to respond to slaps and water douches. The crowd of whispering onlookers, who you know would hang you should it ever reach court. When they do eventually come around, looking like waking babies, relief is instant and you swear to yourself that you'll 'never do it again'; but you know you will.

Murder. When you just say it, when you pluck the word out of the air like a tossed coin, it says and means very little. Someone kills someone else. Just a single word that, which until it happens to you or the possibility of it, lays detached from reality, with no real meaning or depth. When you've killed someone, or think you might have, the word becomes fear and diarrhoea-inducing.

I've waited, like a prisoner on death row, for many a unconscious foe to come around, watching my own life fall away before my very eyes.

It's not just a case of John killing Frank, John goes to prison, Frank goes to the morgue. Along with John's liberty goes the house he's worked so hard for, his girlfriend/wife who can't wait the twenty year jail term for him, his children's youth, and his children. His friends, possibly his family, all his belongings, his self-respect and probably, worst of all, his piece of mind. The list goes on. Possibly and probably, John loses everything.

When (if) he eventually does come out of jail, he's often a broken man, even unsure of where he stands in the hereafter. John's family are haunted by the press, ignored by the neighbours, threatened by Frank's family and friends. They become social outcasts, often even taking the blame for what's happened firmly on their own shoulders. The subsequent pressure takes years off their lives.

When Frank dies, his family are of course devastated. His young wife has a breakdown from which she never really recovers. Mum cries day and night because the last time she saw Frank, she scolded him for his heavy drinking. His brothers spend the next umpteen years living only for revenge, the obsession placing pressure on their own marriages or relationships, causing arguments and often split-ups.

John's life is over – not just Frank's – and both families, who are the real victims, never really recover, their lives changed irreversibly and immeasurably.

Before and during an altercation you don't think of these things, only afterwards does the cold bill of reality drop through the letterbox of your mind.

As you can see, I think about it all deeply, and the constant thought is becoming a great weakness.

To be an effective fighter/doorman you have, at times, to be devoid of such emotions because they cause indecision, and indecision begets defeat. Then you become Frank instead of John. Karate teaches, as does life, that you should learn to transcend fighting, it's a sign of maturity, but that same maturity can, as I've mentioned, cause indecision etc. So, it's a choice between the devil and the deep blue sea. You don't want to fight, but if you don't you'll lose and possibly die. If you do fight you may win but possibly kill.

Either way you lose. I've always believed that it's better to be judged by twelve than carried by six. I still hold on to that belief, but only by the skin of my teeth. The best way, of course, is to avoid confrontations like the plague, but when violence follows you through life like an unwanted smell it's not easy, but we have to try.

D, 'the Karate Kid', as he was commonly known in the Devon pub, due to the fact that he held a black belt in kung fu, had barely transcended idiocy, never mind fighting. He was the kind of man that you couldn't dislike – until you got to know him.

He saw violence in a romantic way. A lot of people who haven't experienced the horrors of real fighting imagine it to be like celluloid fisticuffs, with a hero, a baddie and tomato-ketchup blood.

When they 'feel' the real thing it usually appalls them, but, until that first feel, there's no telling them. As the Chinese say, feeling is believing.

Napoleon Bonaparte once said that there is nothing like the sight of a battlefield after the fight to inspire princes with a love of peace and a hate of war.

The Karate Kid had not yet seen his 'battlefield', but the way he was going he would soon; very soon. He walked like a fighter, talked like a fighter and by fuck he knew he was a fighter. He was tall with a lean, muscular, athletic frame, and handsome features set under a cap of short dark hair, and always five o'clock-shadowed, and a walk, what a walk. All he needed was a set of spurs and a six gun and the picture would have been complete. I was reliably informed that he once had an arse-hole transplant . . . and it rejected him.

Having worked the Devon door for two years, I had, of course, noticed the Karate Kid and sensed his arrogance, a by-product of overconfidence, but I took little notice of him. I didn't like him much and I wasn't alone on that count. That was until one Tuesday night in cold October, when his over-zealous overconfidence over-flowed into an insult that aimed itself in my direction.

'Would you mind seeing your drinks off, please?' I asked the Kid who was strutting his wares on the pinball machine.

'Fuck off, can't you see I'm playin'?' he replied, without taking his eyes from the game. His tall, skinny, weasel-faced friend smiled. He was dressed in a scabby black T-shirt and dirty blue jeans, and was clearly impressed by his friend's brave comment.

'I don't fucking care what ya' doin',' I returned, equally acidic, 'just see your drink off.'

I then turned to his smiling mate whose smarmy 'fuck off' smile bothered me lots. 'ALL RIGHT?' I challenged. His smile fell into a frown. I think he got the message.

Actually this incident reminds me of a time outside Busters nightclub many years ago when I'd knocked a chap out cold for calling me a cock-sucker. I wouldn't mind but I've never sucked a cock in my life. Honest! His mate, obviously upset by his friend's sudden and unexpected unconsciousness jumped right in front of me, arms splayed, chest pushed forward, mouth locked in a growl, snarling, 'YEAH? *Yeah?*' His body language was aggressive, but more specifically the fact that he had dropped into single syllables told me that I was about to be smacked. The syllable used can be one of many, 'yeah', 'all right', 'and', or 'so'. They are often followed/combined with a glare, a nod of the head or splayed-out arms and are actually challenges to engage in a fight. Mostly the verbal challenge, whichever one it may be, is followed very quickly by a physical attack. It's a subliminal trigger-action.

In the prize ring the boxer leads with his jab, he uses it to set up the big right. You know this, so you learn to parry the jab and so avoid the right. The street fighter uses dialogue as his leading attack, words like 'yeah', 'and', 'so', to set you up for his big right, if you don't understand this then you cannot defend against it and you become just another victim. If you are in the game you'd better learn the language.

Unbeknown to me, Colin, my fellow doorman, was watching the fight from the office camera. He'd watched me knock out the first one and now watched again as I knocked out the second. The one who'd called 'yeah'. He rushed out of the office to the front door to give me a piece of his mind. His face black with a Jamaican suntan turned red with rage. He pointed to the two unconscious men on the floor but kept his angry eyes on me.

'Why did you knock the second one out Geoff?'

I thought for a second. Then I felt a little silly because 'yeah' as a single word didn't seem enough reason for knocking someone unconscious.

'He, well . . . he said . . . he said, "yeah",' I stammered. It sounded bad. I knew it would.

'You can't 'spark' someone for saying "yeah",' Colin shouted angrily. I imagined standing in court with some old coffin-dodger rubbing his well-groomed chin and saying 'So Mr Thompson. Run this one by me again because I'm not sure that I heard you correctly, why did you knock this man unconscious?'

'Because he said "yeah", and I don't like people calling me "Yeah".'

When I'd finally calmed Colin down I explained to him and he seemed to understand. If you don't know the language and that 'yeah', 'and', 'so', etc will usually be followed by an attack, you'll get hurt. You have to translate what has been said and then attack before they do. But don't expect it to stand up in court. The judge is very unlikely to have read the 'real' script.

I digress. Back to the Karate Kid.

The Karate Kid remained quiet and carried on playing pinball. I walked away before my temper got the better of me and then him.

'I'm gonna give that wanker 'car park rash' if he doesn't watch his mouth.'

Alan laughed. He didn't like him either. Two years ago I'd have probably blasted him for his ignorance and cheek, but the mature Geoff let it slip, gave a second chance, held off the sentence. I thought that with my 'rep' as a half-decent karate man in the city, my friend would have had a little respect and given me a wide berth. But he obviously didn't have any respect for me.

The atmosphere between us over the next couple of months was strained to say the least. Every week I'd ask him politely to 'drink up' and he'd ignore me. It went on and on like this for a while. I guess I should have said something and nipped it in the bud. But I was trying to avoid a scene, not because of fear – other than the fear that I might kill him if I started – but rather because I was desperately trying to transcend violence. I wasn't going to do that by whacking everyone who got a little cheeky. He obviously thought my reluctance was due to trepidation because with each passing week he got braver and braver. The final inevitable straw came on a November Sunday evening. The pub was as busy as usual. Sundays are notoriously slow to empty at the end of the night. People seem to think that by grabbing on to a few extra moments at closing time they will delay the inevitable Monday morning feeling that awaits them as soon as their heads hit the pillow.

The long lounge was heaving with bodies of both sexes (oh! yes please!) all ages, colours and creeds. The bar staff were walking around collecting glasses and wiping tables, trying to squeeze between slow-drinking punters. Smoke collected above heads like fog. One of the doormen opened the exit doors to let in a little cold. This was our way of hinting to customers that it's 'time to go'. As I walked around I talked and joked with friends and strangers alike. I bent down by the side of a beautiful girl in a wheel chair, once a brilliant athlete paralysed in a freak car accident. She was very gorgeous and I kissed her on the cheek. She blushed and brushed back her silky auburn hair, I hugged her face close to mine, she smelt of expensive perfume and roses (actually I made the roses bit up, I thought it sounded nice).

'You're gorgeous, you are,' I told her. She smiled.

'You're spoiling me,' she said shyly.

'You need spoiling,' I said laughingly as I continued my walk around the pub. One of the glass collectors, a cheeky little fucker, walked past with hands full of glasses. He nudged into me.

'Get out of my way you poof!' he said jokingly. I grabbed him around the neck and started to strangle him, albeit very gently.

'A young man with his hands full shouldn't be so fucking cheeky,' I hissed into his ear, then I bit as though I was going to tear it off. When he yelped I let him go and started laughing. But he made sure that he was a safe distance away from me before he shouted:

'Next time poof!'

The Karate Kid was strutting as usual. He was by the bar with his friends. I asked him to drink up. He blanked me, and I blanked him, blanking me. I collected a few glasses and squeezed through the crowds, making my way to the bar. In a fit of arrogance the Karate Kid stood in my way, blocking my path to the bar. For a second I contemplated feeding him a glass, but knew that wouldn't be fair, some poor barmaid would have to clean up the mess. He nodded his head sardonically, like one of those nodding dogs in the back of a car. His chest swelled in his black cotton, cap-sleeve T-shirt. Very seventies, I thought.

He'd gone a little too far this time and to be honest I'd had enough of his arrogance so I pushed him out of my way with my shoulder. I immediately felt his angry eyes burning into the back of my head as I passed him. I smiled nervously to myself. On the way back from the bar the silly fucker stood in my way again. I was very close to giving him a right hook but settled for the shoulder push again. I barged him much harder this time so that he stumbled right back. His eyes nearly popped out of their sockets. As I strolled away from him I turned and smiled, then gave a little wink. My stomach began its customary pre-fight churn as my paranoid, over-active adrenal gland went into action. I kept my face even, so as not to show him my build-up. He showed everyone his by staring holes in me. He clenched and unclenched his fists like an amateur. I could tell he hadn't done much by this display, but that didn't stop him from being potentially dangerous. I knew now that there was going to be a lot of trouble and it was my own fault for not stopping this thing when it first started. It's always the same though, you give a man an inch and he'll take a mile. Well I was sick of him now, he'd pushed me too far, and he was going to have to have some. I had to be a bit careful though, he was a black belt after all, and apparently he was quite good. It is never good form to underestimate an opponent; no matter how big an arse-hole they've made of themselves. Alan, big at five foot ten and fourteen stone, and with short greying hair, listened as I told him about the incident. As we spoke I noticed out of the corner of my eye that the Karate Kid had cornered Seymour, the head doorman. They talked urgently, then looked my way.

'Sort it out, Sey,' I heard him say aggressively as they parted. Seymour approached Alan and me. He was an excellent doorman with many years of experience. Anyone this man had not fought in his time was not worth talking about. He was also a real gentleman. He was always immaculately smart with heavy gold jewellery and an Omega watch. A broken nose, the badge of battle hereabouts, centred his roguish Jamaican face. He leaned in towards Alan and myself.

'Have you had any trouble with the Karate Kid?'

My adrenaline went into overdrive. This was it.

'Yeah. I 'ave Sey. Why, wot's 'e said?'

Seymour shrugged his shoulders. 'He didn't actually say it was you Geoff, but he was talking 'fighting talk'.' Seymour's voice fell into Jamaican slang at the end of each sentence, especially when fighting was mentioned.

'Does he want to 'speak' to me then, Sey?' I asked, knowing the answer.

'Yeah, I think so.'

As soon as Sey spoke I went into fight-mode. I walked toward the open exit doors where he was standing like a proud cock with his mate the weasel and a couple of young ladies. My adrenaline rose higher, but I had no problem controlling it because I was so PISSED OFF. I was so angry that this fucking lemon was forcing me to be physical when I was so desperately trying not to. You see, my problem is that I can take a lot of shit and hold myself back quite well, but, when I 'go' I really do 'go', and I find it hard to stop myself. I fear this lack of control will one day get me into a lot of trouble.

What was about to happen was so unnecessary. He'd placed me in a position where I felt I had to fight. If I didn't I would lose face badly. Every time you let someone off with a disrespectful act it chips away at your power base. Let it happen too often and you no longer have a power base at all. Without it you can't do the job you're paid to do because people won't let you if they have no respect for you.

Several other people looked on as I moved closer to the Karate Kid. He was fidgeting on the spot and nodding his head, breathing heavily and staring right through me. These were the signs of unrestrained fear. An experienced fighter would never let them show.

'You wanna speak wi' me?' I asked firmly.

'Yeah, I do actually,' he answered, in an attempt to be hard.

'Come out, let's talk,' I beckoned as I walked a few feet into the car park. He followed. He was like a lamb to the mint sauce. As he approached he began to angle his body sideways, as though he was lining me up with a kick, though I couldn't be sure. It didn't matter anyway, I'd already decided that he was going to have some. I'd spent two months trying to avoid it and was fed up with trying. I'd made a mistake. I'd let him get away with too much and now I was about to redress the problem. I had no more chances left in my chance bag.

As he got closer his face began to grimace and I sensed an impending attack.

BANG!

Almost in slow motion, I dropped a heavy right on his jaw. It shuddered with the impact. As he fell, I volleyed his face and he spiralled down. I kicked him so hard my foot hurt. I felt weeks of anger leaving my body. He landed face-down on the tarmac of defeat. Many people were watching, so I thought I'd give them a display. Not for ego or malice, I just wanted to take out a little insurance, make the onlookers think that I was an animal. In the future this would ensure that they didn't tangle with me. The Chinese call it killing a chicken to train a monkey.

'KIAAA!' I let out a fearsome shout as I brought an axe-kick into his side. To the onlooker, it probably looked barbaric, which is how I wanted it to look, but in reality, the kick was empty. I pulled it on impact, just as I had thousands of times before in training.

The man with the weasel face ran at me with ill intent. I stopped him in his tracks with a lash of my tongue.

'GER OUT 'F MY FUCKING FACE BEFORE I DESTROY YA!'

He stopped dead. The crowd of onlookers murmured. Seymour tried to pick the Karate Kid off the floor where he lay lifeless. As I walked past, his face was about waist height, so I back-heeled it, again just for show. It had the desired effect because as I re-entered the pub somebody shouted, 'Fucking animal!'

Don't you just hate flattery?

Several glances met mine as I walked back into the pub. The beautiful girl in the wheel chair's eyes bored into me, as though she were looking at me for the very first time. She looked shocked, and disappointed. Which made me feel a little sad. Kenny, the body-builder, joined the several desperately trying to find the Karate Kid's lost consciousness. It was obviously very well hidden, because no one seemed to be able to find it. I watched from the door with growing horror as the lump of body refused to move.

'Wake up you bastard,' I cried inside. 'Wake up!' My nightmare had begun.

Several would-be first-aiders also tried, but to no avail. Kenny, a pocket Hercules with a painted-on smile, moved into have a go.

'Good,' I thought, 'Kenny will get him round, he's done this loads of times.' But no. The Karate Kid was having none of it.

His companions were beginning to panic. They talked of hospitals and police and the likes. In the end, three of them picked him up, still unconscious, and carried him to a waiting car. The toes of his shoes dragged and scuffed across the car park. He definitely didn't look healthy. The makeshift ambulance, an orange Mini, sped from the car park, leaving me mentally hanging from the ceiling by my fingernails. I felt certain in my mind that he was dead, and by the look of Kenny, Alan and Seymour, they thought so too. I shook my head. Why the fuck did I kick him? Why didn't I just knock him out and leave it at that? If you kill somebody with a single punch, you may have some chance of defence in court. But if you've hoofed his head in as well, while he's out, especially while he's out, you might as well stick your head between your legs and kiss your arse good-bye. So many witnesses too.

I thought about Sharon at home in bed, her supple warmth beckoning me, and suddenly I had to be with her. A shadow darkened over my heart and I felt very low,

I had to go home to Sharon, to hold her, be with her. If he's dead, what will I do? How will she cope? She'll lose the house, there's no way she could afford to keep it alone.

Alan lay sleeplessly on his pine double bed, his brown, sinewy body glistened in the moonlight that stole through the window of his third-floor Woodend flat. Al felt sure that the Karate Kid was dead and it bothered him. He'd seen unconscious people before, but not like this. This time there was no blood or gore, he just looked dead. His face was blue and his body jellied, he must have been out ten minutes before they took him to hospital. He knew I was going to take him out, he deserved it too, he just wished that Geoff, the hair-trigger, hadn't been quite so severe.

Kenny lay on the single bed in his own room at his mother's terraced house half-way down a tree-lined street in Wyken, a nicer part of the city. He could have slept but saw no point, he was pretty sure that he was going to be arrested tonight. After all, he was one of the last people to touch the 'body'. Ken had seen hundreds of unconscious people and had, in his time, become a bit of a 'whizz' at bringing them around, but not the Karate Kid. He'd told me at the time, that he thought the K.K. was all right, just to ease my mind, but secretly he believed that the Karate Kid was in a bad way, as bad at least as any he'd seen in all of his eight years on the door. He breathed in a deep sigh, almost smacking himself in the face with his huge barrel chest.

I had, in all the years I'd known Ken, never seen him without a smile on his face, he reminded me of Batman's 'the Joker'. Ken was one of the most respected doormen in the city. He was also one of the biggest wind-up merchants too. If you let him he'd have you in tears; telling you that your girlfriend was sleeping around, that you were looking fat when you were trying to lose weight, thin when you were trying to gain weight. Or that the good-looking girl you fancy is a 'tramp' with more conquests than Chris Bonnington. 'She's nice Ken,' you'd say, pointing to a good-looker. 'She's a 'tramp',' he'd reply, reeling off a list of men who'd slept with her. And it didn't matter who you were, if you were in the company you'd be having some.

At twelve thirty a.m. the front doorknocker on Kenny's house nearly had him jumping out of his skin. He ran and looked out of the bedroom window.

SHIT! There was a copper waiting at the door.

As I drove back along the deserted streets to my house I pondered on what a lonely place the world could be. I thought too about the mess I was in and the bigger mess my life would become if the Karate Kid popped his socks. I was living a nightmare. In court I wouldn't stand a maggot-on-hook's chance of surviving. Everything was against me.

Trying to satisfy a judge that I was innocent would be like trying to convince a white mouse that a black cat was lucky. I had more chance of nailing jelly to the ceiling.

I pulled into the cul-de-sac where my house lay. I parked the car, made my way up the garden path and into the temporary sanctuary of my home. I didn't expect to be here for long before I was arrested.

Kenny opened the bedroom window slightly, preparing himself to hear the bad news, he was sure now that he was about to be arrested. From the top the policeman's head looked like a huge tit, and Kenny wondered if his head went right to the top of it. The door was still not answered, so the policeman knocked again more determinedly.

Sharon was in bed when I got home. Sometimes she waited up for me, other times, if she was really tired, she'd go upstairs and fall asleep watching the portable telly. I made my way up the stairs and entered the bedroom. Sharon was tucked snugly under the covers like a little baby. The whole room was a glow of memories and warmth. Was I going to lose her after tonight – forever – because of a wanker they called the Karate Kid?

I lay still fully-clothed on the bed next to Sharon. I could smell her white musk perfume, felt the radiating warmth emitting from her body, and sensed the despair she would taste when I was gone.

Being separated by prison to someone as close as us would be like death.

Now, I lay next to my beautiful, smooth-skinned, lovely Sharon. Tomorrow I could be sharing a bunk with a farting, burping, hairy-arsed villain with a face like an ugly caveman's. The thought made me shudder. I cuddled up to my lady. She half awoke and held me tight. What the fuck had I done?

My body craved sleep but alas my bed was one of nettles and my mind had gone into overdrive, so there was little chance. I kissed Sharon gently on her soft lips. Aren't they always that much softer when you think you're kissing them for the last time? I ran my fingers gently through her dark, short, soft hair and wondered whether this would be the last time I'd get to do this.

Her tired eyes opened to greet me then closed again involuntarily, making her look much younger than her twenty-one years. And vulnerable, she looked so vulnerable. Who would take care of her when I was away? Who would make her laugh, cradle her to sleep at night, love and need her? My mates would probably be queuing up when I was out of the way, mates are like that. She needed me. She was independent and strong, but I knew she'd grown to need me. I thought of my beautiful children who doted on me. Kerry, who spent hours late at night conversing with me on anything and everything. Lisa, beautiful Lisa, who loved to jog with me at weekends, hit the ball in my garage gym and push hands when the others were watching telly. Jennie, she never leaves my side, following me everywhere, and not really talking, just linking on to me, holding me. Then there was Louis, whose wavy blond hair, deep, cavernous blue eyes and red, chubby face enchanted me, and his constant barrage of three-year-old questions, 'Why, daddy, why?'

How would they be without me and me without them?

Life without Sharon, without my kids, without my freedom, was definitely not 'life'. To assuage my fears I tried to convince myself that the Karate Kid was all right and indeed not D.O.A., but the omniscient Mr Negative inside me was having none of it. I wasn't about to get off that easily.

I decided as I always do in situations like this, that if I was going to come to terms with what I'd done and the possible consequences and thus get a little sleep, I was going to have to accept those consequences. The only way to do this was ask myself, 'What was the worst possible thing that could happen in this situation?' Then answer myself honestly, 'I could go to prison.' I then put my mind into the highest gear it would go into and tell myself that, 'I can handle that.' If the worst comes to the worst and he dies and I inevitably go to prison, 'I could handle it'. Your mind is a funny old tool, filled at times of stress with the negative, always looking on the black side of things.

I gently shook Sharon to wake her up, then told her of my problem and that I expected to be arrested that night. I suggested that she should be strong. She nodded sleepily and I cradled her off to sleep.

My imagination wandered as sleep beckoned. In my dreams I was cuffed to a 'rozzer' in an echoey courtroom, where the Karate Kid's friends and family stood in judgement. The judge, jury and executioner, pointing and moaning in haunting voices, 'Animal! Animal! Animal!'

UUHH! I woke up with a start in a cold sweat.

I thought for a moment about the courts and judges. I know someone has to rule this fair land of ours and I understand that they should, for obvious reasons, be educated. But why are they always so detached from reality? They have absolutely no conception of the 'real world', the one outside of the courtroom. They don't know the language nor the body talk of the 'street'. They don't know that when someone hostile says 'yeah!' they mean, 'Yeah, do you wanna go?' Or if they splay their hands erratically, lurch their neck forward like a pecking hen, or turn sideways on to you, it means that they are preparing to attack. Or that when a good fighter says that he doesn't want to fight you it normally means that he does want to fight you, he's just disarming you before engagement. If he smirks and nods his head he's subliminally calling you 'a wanker'. If you ask him to 'leave the club' or 'behave' and he doesn't answer, or worse still if he very slowly looks you up and down and then doesn't answer, he's telling you that he respects you so little that you don't even warrant a reply. There are so many ways that a person can throw down the gauntlet without actually saying 'let's fight' and each in its own right demands a response if 'face' is to be saved. Many of these people have no conception of real life or the trappings of a working class whose unwritten scripture says that 'if you don't fight – if you can't fight – you're fucked.

Again I digress to the soapbox. Anyway, I'd got my head around prison, but sleep was still eluding me. My ears seemed to prick like an alert Alsatian, picking up every sound and movement like a radio antenna. I could hear Sharon's soft breathing, the clang of the central heating, the distant call of motorway car engines, the hum of nearby electricity cables, even the fast staccato of my own heart beat was starting to 'cabbage' me. 'Fuck me!' I wanted to shout to all the inanimate objects. 'Can't you see I'm trying to sleep?' I desperately listened for the crack of police boots on my footpath. Bastards! All those biscuits and coffees I'd given them over the years as well. I listened too for the ring of the phone saying, 'He's dead, he's dead, he's dead'. Even the fluttering leaves of the conifers that I'd tended so lovingly seemed to join in unison with the wind.

'He's dead, he's dead, he's dead.'

Then, the very neighbours' cat that I left saucers of milk for, getting all his mates in my garden:

'Miaow, he's dead, he's dead, miaow.'

KNOCK!

HUH? I awoke with a start. Was that the door?

The policeman stood waiting at Kenny's door. The tension was killing Ken. He contemplated shouting to his mum to answer the bloody door, but he didn't need to, the door was opened, and his mother greeted the awaiting policeman.

'Sorry to bother you madam, but is that your Cortina?'

He pointed to a beige car on the road outside the house. Kenny's mum looked and so did Ken. 'No, it belongs to the Campbells next door.'

'No problem, he's left his sidelights on that's all, I'll give him a knock, save his battery.'

'PHEW! Thank fuck for that,' thought Kenny as he jumped back into bed.

I sat up with a jerk, woken by the knock, from the restless sleep to which nature had condemned me. Was that the door? The police? A friend delivering bad news? I looked for the time on the electric clock on the small bedside table beside Sharon. There was no clock. It lay forlorn and upturned on the carpet from when Sharon had rolled in her sleep and knocked it off. I tried to recapture the lost sleep. If I could last the night without being arrested, I'd be home free. If he were dead or comatose, I'd have been arrested by now. I unashamedly clasped my hands and prayed to God for forgiveness and a fifty-first chance. Sleep overcame me almost a second later, and, all too soon, morning arrived. As soon as I awoke, the previous night's fears were back, perched on the shoulder of my mind's eye but to a slightly lesser degree. I'd survived the night without arrest, which was a good sign.

All the same, I switched my radio on to local Mercia for the news, then Harmony for their news, then CWR. When bad news was not forthcoming, I switched to Radio 1 to see if 'Batesy' had heard anything. Apparently not. Sharon gave me plenty of comforting hugs, telling me it would be all right. After I'd dropped her off at work, I decided to go and see Al, he'd put my mind at rest.

'I thought he was dead Geoff.' (Well maybe not.)

Seeing the dismay his words had caused he retreated, with, 'Though I'm sure he's not, you'd have heard by now.' (Too late Al, the damage is done.) Though he did say the Karate Kid was a wanker and needed some pain. I knew that.

We switched on the telly for a bit of light relief only to find that every channel was doing talks, plays and films about violence and death, displaying vignettes of brutality and going into the histrionics of how easily somebody could be killed by a kick to the head. I turned the telly off and turned instead to a cup of tea, which helped somewhat.

The city arcade was a wind tunnel as a northerly gust ran through it like an icy gauntlet, blowing anything and everything this way and that, except my hair, which was tightly concealed under my leather Fila hat. I hadn't much hair left due to hereditary receding, one good gust of wind and I could be completely bald, which wouldn't do.

The arcade held a scattering of people who dared to brave the winter chill. I made my way to the end of the arcade where the 'newspaper man' stood, his eyes hidden amid a thousand wrinkles, mouth lost in a walrus moustache. His head was veiled under a chequered, ill-fitting cap that met and matched the lapels of an overcoat that swept the floor as he walked. Every now and then his mouth would emerge from its hiding place under the uncut 'tache like a gaping hole in a walker's welly.

'AAUUU!' came the inaudible sales pitch. Roughly translated it meant 'Telegraph', or if it was an evening edition of the paper, 'CIIFO!' which meant 'City Final'. There were about ten of these lovely characters scattered all around the city centre, selling the 'Coventry Evening Telegraph' from portable kiosks. I bought twenty-five pence worth of 'AAUUU', to see if I was headlining or whether my imagination was just playing a cruel, unfunny joke on me. I scanned every page. My heart jumped when I saw the headline, 'Local Man Murdered'.

I read the story as quickly as I could, in between gusts of wind blowing the pages into my eyes. My hands shook with trepidation. I stumbled over the words, scanning for my name, hoping it wasn't there.

It wasn't me. I threw my head back in relief. It wasn't me. It was someone murdered in a domestic incident in neighbouring Bedworth.

I sat in my neat, clean, furnished front room staring at the telephone. I wanted to pick it up and ring the Devon to see if they'd heard anything, but I dared not. What if they had and it was 'bad'? That was the last thing I wanted to hear. On the other hand, it could be good news. I decided to ring. I'd have to find out sooner or later. The dull tring at the end of my earpiece seemed to go on forever. Every ring sent waves down to my churning stomach.

Ring, ring. Ring, ring. (Come on ya bastard, answer the phone.)

'Hello?' said the disembodied voice at the other end of the line. It was Jim, our gentleman boss at the Devon.

'Hello Jim, it's Geoff.' There was a cold silence. 'Have you heard anything?'

'Well,' he said, pausing momentarily, prolonging my agony, 'hold on a minute Geoff, let me take the call in my office. Hold on a sec'.' The distance between the bar and the office was, at the most five feet, so why did it take Jim about three hours and twenty minutes to get there? Why? Time distortion; that's why. I don't know what I've ever done to offend this omniscient tactician of pain, but I must have done something very bad because he certainly had it in for me. Eventually Jim came back on the line.

'He hasn't been in Geoff, but as far as I can tell, he's all right. One of the locals said he'd seen him out and about.'

Relief filled my body.

'One of the locals 'as seen him you say?' I asked, wanting the good news re-affirmed, in case my ears had deceived me.

'Yeah, anyway, you'd have heard by now if he wasn't,' he said as an afterthought.

If I was brothers with Stress, I was definitely shagging Relief, because it did feel nice. 'Yahoo!' I wanted to shout. So I did, but felt a right twat afterwards and decided not to do it again, unless the neighbours thought I'd lost my marbles.

In the spacious porch of the Devon, looking out on to the large car park, Alan, Kenny, Seymour and I laughed and joked about how we were all sure that the Karate Kid was dead and how our imaginations had run wild.

'He was in earlier on Geoff,' Kenny said. 'Well, I say he was in, but actually he wouldn't get out of the car. He was shitting himself in case you gave it to him again. He was as nervous as fuck. He asked whether you were in yet. I told him you'd be in later.'

'I'm just fucking glad he's not dead,' I said. All the lads laughed, they shared my relief. They'd all been there before. Kenny continued:

'I told him you wouldn't do anything Geoff. I 'ad to, he looked like he was gonna cry.'

We all laughed again.

About an hour later the Karate Kid drove into the car park in a battered purple Capri. He wound the window down. I was by the door. Even from there I could see he was crapping himself. His fear was almost tangible.

His voice was capitulating, 'Can I have a word with you please?'

'Yeah, sure.'

I could see that he was scared and I didn't want to tear the arse out of it so I put him at ease by talking nicely. This is my way.

'Sorry about the other night,' he offered, looking at the floor.

'Forget it, it's done, I'm not a man to hold a grudge, as far as I'm concerned it's over.'

He shrugged again. 'I'm sorry.' He paused. 'Am I barred? All my mates drink in here, I'd hate to be barred.'

I patted him on the arm sympathetically.

'As far as I'm concerned, it's forgotten, you can come back into the pub and we can be friends.' His eyes lit up.

'Really? I'd like that.'

We parted on a handshake and I sighed deeply and thought, 'There but for the grace of God, go I.'

4. Three Card Bluff

You can call someone's bluff once and if you're lucky and cheeky, even twice, but three times is just taking the piss.

Mr R had fallen for my bluff twice, and considering that he was a hugely violent man, who'd made a career out of hurting people, I was more than a little surprised the first two times.

The first time I called his bluff was in the late eighties, when violence in Coventry pubs was the norm and I was at my aggressive best. Basically, I asked him to leave an establishment, as he held a life ban for petrol bombing the place a couple of years earlier (detailed in *Watch My Back*). He refused, I challenged him to a fight, and he backed down and left. The second time was four years later, not long after he'd been released from jail where he was serving time for much violence and aggravation. Again, I found myself in a position where I had to ask him to leave the establishment in which I was working, a place different from the first, but for the same reason from which he also had a life ban. In fact he was so violent that he carried life bans from most of the pubs and clubs in Coventry. The only ones that didn't ban him were the places where the landlords were too scared to do so.

As I'd bluffed him the first time I thought I'd try the same ploy again, after all, at sixteen stone he was a bit of a monster, so if at all possible fighting was best avoided.

The Lion was a grand Edwardian pub sitting proudly in its own large car park just off a main city road. Situated in the popular and quiet Coventry suburb of Walsgrave, it had a lovely, castle-like church to its immediate right. Bill, or 'Willmot-Brown' as the regulars called him (on account of his uncanny likeness to the infamous villain in the popular soap, *Eastenders*), was temporarily in charge of the Lion. I was working at the Devon at the time but because I liked Bill and because I knew that he wasn't a fighter, I'd promised to 'look after him' for his short duration at the pub.

'Any trouble Bill, just ring me and I'll sort it out for you,' I told him. Of course, when you make this kind of offer, no matter how well meaning it is, you never really expect to be taken up on it.

Anyway, on a Sunday afternoon, a lovely cooked dinner sitting comfortably in my belly, I was sitting on a commodious settee and readying myself for an afternoon of 'eye-exercising' in front of the telly. The phone rang.

'Let the answer machine take it, Geoff,' shouted Sharon, who was washing up the dinner dishes in the kitchen. I might have done if it was switched on, but it wasn't, so I picked up the phone.

I knew there was trouble because Bill always gave a big sigh before he gave you bad news. He sounded worried on the other end of the line.

'Mr R's in Geoff, I've asked him to leave but he won't have it.'

I cursed myself for not having had the answer machine on.

'OK,' I said, hiding the build-up of adrenaline, 'I'm on my way.'

When I arrived there was a police car already outside the pub; someone must have rung them, though nobody knew whom. Bill was talking to one of them. I hoped, as

I left the comfort and safety of my car, that the knuckle-duster swinging at the bottom of my pocket wasn't too obvious. Apparently, Mr R was in the bar with four others, so an 'equaliser' was necessary, just in case.

'Geoff's gonna get him out,' Bill confidently told the police, who seemed keen to get in there themselves. They hated him too, said he was a horrible bastard who should be in a permanent state of 'lock-up'. He had, in his time, demolished several coppers, so was very low on their popularity list. On this lovely Sunday afternoon in February, when I should have been at home, wallowing and being fussed by my lady, I have to tell you that he was even lower on mine. I got my head into fight-mode, and screwed my face up like chewed toffee in readiness for my confrontation. Aggressively, I pushed through the double doors and into the pub, a huge room with a circular bar right in the centre. Pool tables were on the left and a D.J. consul to the extreme right. The place was full to bursting with Sunday morning drinkers. All eyes were riveted on me as I burst through the doors. Mr R sat between four hard, scarred-faced associates on a run of red leather wall-seating behind three tables of drinks. Mr R looked up at me, as did his followers. I met each stare individually. I drilled holes in them. None met the challenge, all eyes dropped to the table like a bad hand of cards.

I looked at Mr R. He had a hard, dark face capped by a crown of thick black hair. His small, fat nose was underlined by a thick black moustache. If I had a nose like that I wouldn't underline it. My extreme show of confidence and scowling face obviously did the trick because he accepted my invitation to leave the premises with little hesitation. When I whipped the leather baseball cap off my head and tossed it across the room in an aggressive, challenging manner, he left without demur. There was an almost audible sigh of relief from the other customers. I enjoyed a celebratory bottle of beer. This was the second and I hoped the last confrontation with Mr R. The next four weeks saw a Mr R-free Lion, and temporarily, I forgot all about him.

Sharon had been poorly all week with a stomach bug. Over the last couple of weeks all my family had had the bug, so, I concluded, and rightly so, that diarrhoea 'runs in your jeans'. Anyway, by the Thursday her appetite was returning and her stomach was being a little less fussy, and not catapulting food out as soon as it came in. As a little treat for my lady I cooked a lovely spaghetti. It went down and stayed down very well. I rested on the settee in a bid to let the food settle. It was early on the Thursday evening.

BRRRR, BRRRR. The phone buzzed into life.

'Let the answer machine take it,' said Sharon, from the kitchen where she was doing some domestic engineering.

Bastard, it wasn't on again.

'Hello?' I said, trying at the same time to watch *The Bill* on the television out of the corner of my eye. The heavy sigh told me that it was Bill and that it was trouble. The spaghetti turned over in my stomach like a spun cocktail.

'Our friend's back. And he's got a mate with him, some Scotch guy from Woodend.'

'Is anyone else there?' I asked, meaning the other doormen.

'I phoned Les, he said to ring you.'

'OK, is he on his way down?'

'Yeah, I think so.'

'Right. I'll be down in a minute.' Sharon looked across the room at me.

'Trouble?'

I shrugged my shoulders and nodded.

'It's that fucking Mr R again, 'e's in the Lion and 'e won't leave.'

'Where are the other doormen Geoff? It's a Thursday night, they must have doormen on.' It was a valid point, but I didn't know the answer. I shrugged again.

'There can't be any on or 'e wouldn't 'ave rung me.' I sat down and tightly laced my leather Fila trainers. These were my fighting shoes. Adrenaline shot into the unexpected mass of spaghetti Bolognese still digesting in my stomach. I wondered whether I might be seeing it again, very soon.

I decided to try and bluff Mr R again, but I knew in my heart of hearts that this time he wouldn't go for it, this time we'd be fighting. My hands shook as I zipped up my black Fila tracksuit top and put on my dark baseball cap which had the initials *G.T.* embroidered in yellow across the top. I walked to the front door, ready to leave. Sharon jumped up from her seat and called me back.

'Come here,' she said, with a hint of sadness in her voice. She wrapped her arms around me tightly and squeezed. She knew I'd be fighting this time too.

'Be careful Geoff, you know what he's like. Will you ring me when it's done?' She looked into my eyes as she spoke.

'Yeah, all right, but if I get stabbed to death,' I said with my very own kind of black humour, 'don't you kiss any other boys for at least a fortnight.' I laughed as she slapped my shoulder.

'Don't talk like that Geoff, you know I don't like it. You're sick.' I smiled and kissed her gently on the lips then walked to my car. Half-way down the path Sharon said with a tease in her voice, 'You know I'd wait at least three weeks.'

I laughed as I got into the car and drove off.

Three days before, a friend and fellow doorman had been killed by a single stab wound to the heart outside a nightclub in the city centre. When his convulsing frame fell to the pavement, five young men had kicked his dying body again and again and again. He died on the way to hospital. I understood why she was tense. She had every reason to be worried, Mr R had glassed, stabbed, bottled, razored and petrol bombed many before me. He battered old, young, firm, infirm, able and disabled without hesitation or prejudice. A couple of months previously he had shoved a heavy glass ash-tray into the face of the amiable bar-cellar man at the Lion, bludgeoning it into a gaping, bloody wound that needed a hundred stitches and a week in hospital to heal. All for refusing to serve him with a drink.

On the five minute drive to the Lion, I sang to the tune of Elton John's 'Crocodile Rock' reverberating from the car stereo. My voice held the customary pre-fight shake that over the years I'd come to know. It was all part of the build-up. I just ignored it. You learned not to mind it after a while.

The car park was relatively full, so I concluded that the Lion was busy. I parked my car at the front of the pub and walked in through the double red doors. There he was, directly in front of me, standing ten feet away at the bar with his 'Scotch' friend, drinking lager. The adrenaline shot through the spaghetti and filled my chest. I took a deep breath.

As was usual in these situations, all eyes fell upon me as I entered. Everyone knew why I was there and what was about to occur. As I had surmised, the room was full of drinkers. Two old, tortoise-faced men, still dressed in their sixties Sunday best, sat crouched over glasses of slowly depleting beer, talking about 'when I was a lad' and 'the kids today, they don't know they're born'. The beer-pregnant regulars held up the bar, slurring the world's problems to right. Young apprentice slobs knocked the balls around the pool table, bragging about the amount of beer they could drink, and dreaming of one day being 'real' regulars who could drink fifteen pints and still walk home. 'This belly's all paid for,' they'd say, picking up their fat from the belt and juggling it like a bag of spuds. A pretty-faced little girl nick-named 'Five-Two' caught my eye. She was so named because she bet one of the doormen a blow job that she could beat him at pool. She lost five games to two and gave him a little 'head' in the car park. She had the kind of seductive look that made me think that she might have lost on purpose. Whenever she's in there's a huge queue at the pool table to play her. She gave me a wink as I passed. No time for pool today. I took the measure of both men as I approached. Willmot-Brown was nowhere to be seen.

Mr R looked very heavy-set, and was wearing a grey, silky tracksuit and cheap, shiny trainers. His Scotch companion was lighter in weight, though tall, and – well, let's face it – Scottish. With his hard Glasgow accent he could have been eight stone and still have sounded aggressive. His drink-glazed eyes below a cap of blond hair met mine on approach.

I went straight for Mr R with the aggressive approach, but knew my heart wasn't in it. Even before I started I knew he wasn't going to have any of it. I knew I was the absolute cheekiest bastard in the world for even trying, but try I did. I don't like to employ 'physical' unless it's really necessary.

Round the corner of the Lion car park John and Craig, the doormen who were supposed to be working that night, were bent into the boot of Craig's Sierra. They were getting the bats.

Craig was a tough ex-soldier, big at fourteen stone with large hunched shoulders in a permanent state of shrug, and a face that looked in a permanent state of mid-frown with a thick square chin and thinning blond hair, brushed forward to hide the thinning bit. He grabbed two baseball bats from the car, passing one to 'Catalogue' John (he looked like a catalogue model) who stood handsomely at seventeen stone. The bat looked oddly out of place in his hands.

'Lets 'urry up, Geoff should be 'ere in a minute, Willmot said he's rang 'im up.'

Lads, lads, I'm in there already!

'Does he want us to wait for him, then?' asked John, twirling the bat in his hands and nearly dropping it.

'Yeah, 'e said to wait for 'im.'

They walked, bats in hand, back around to the front door of the pub, unaware that I was already inside.

Mr R half-turned as I approached, then turned back to face the bar showing no respect and even less fear. I got straight to the point: 'You've got to leave!'

He turned and met my glance. He must have sensed the lack of commitment in my voice. His beetle-black eyes and hard, empty stare went from me to the nearly-full glass of beer that sat beside him on the bar. He pointed to the said glass, letting me know that he'd got a pint and wasn't leaving. The 'dumb' tactic was an old trick. 'Street-speak' often used by people of his ilk. Its aim is to belittle you, not even showing you enough respect to speak. An attempt at psyching you out. But this was my game. I knew all the rules and all the tricks. His insolence only angered me. I shot again:

'You're barred, you've got to leave.'

He looked at me again, and shook his head. His insolence was frightening because I knew it meant that he was ready to fight.

'It's a new gaff, so I'm not barred.' He slowly lifted the glass to his mouth and drank, then continued. 'I'm not leaving.' Again he turned his back on me. The slur in his voice told me he'd had a few, the tone of his voice told me he wasn't buying my bluff, not today thank you.

'Listen. I'm telling ya'. You've got to leave.'

'No!' he said, arrogantly, and again pointed at his pint. I went for the kill. This would be my last attempt at a 'psych-out'. My feet were already positioned in a small forty-five degree stance, my hands in front as a fence to protect the gap between us. I was ready for the possibility of 'physical'.

'If you don't leave now, we're gonna be fighting.'

And why not? It had worked before, loads of times.

He eyed me suspiciously, looking for any signs of hesitance and fear in my voice. I felt the hesitance and the fear, so I guess it's fair to say that he spotted it too. I didn't mind because it would feed his ego and make him overconfident. I also knew that the more fear I held, the better I would perform, providing I could hold on to it.

My mind stretched back through time in that one second of silence between my challenge and his reply. I remembered the three hundred-plus fights I'd won without defeat over the last eight years of working in this bastard trade. I wondered in a split-second of hesitance whether the law of averages was on my trail and if this would 'the one'. Could this be the time when I lose? In fact, faced by two violent, big men, might I even die? Since my friend had been stabbed and killed I'd thought a lot about life and death. He had been a handy lad, a more-than-capable fighter and now he was dead. I thought about Sharon, who'd been asking me for a while now to start cutting out the door work, and my mum, who worried herself sick about me being involved in violence. Even about Nina, my ex-wife, who'd begged me to leave the profession when we were married. And my kids; was it all worth it?

I crushed the thoughts quickly, as a matter of urgency. 'Then we'll have to fight,' he replied evenly.

Fuck, I never expected that. Scotch turned towards me, his back to the bar, ready to go. I made a mental note of his movement. Mr R turned away from me in a fit of arrogance. I knew I had to hit him and I could sense that any second now that he, or his mate, was going to attack.

The danger was looming fast. The challenge had been thrown and accepted. There was nothing left to do but

fight (or run), and every second that I delayed my pre-
emptive attack would dig a deeper hole for me. I wasn't
just facing one opponent, I was facing two. This was the
hard part, the part where I knew I was going to get
physical, where your legs start to shake and you feel weak.
You even start to doubt yourself and your ability to hurt
your opponents. You feel as though your attacks won't
work, that they'll just bounce off the target like flies off a
windscreen.

'So you're not going to go then?' I said, bringing my
right hand back as though showing the door. This question
gave my brain a chance to engage, and gave my shot a
blind second to land.

Craig and fucking Catalogue John were still waiting
outside the front door for me to arrive, unaware that I
was inside. Willmot-Brown was upstairs in the living
quarters, looking out of the window for me to arrive. I'm
here. *I'm fucking here.* He was probably cursing me for taking
so long.

BANG!

I dropped a heavy right on to Mr R's fat jaw line. I hit
him as hard and as fast as I could. The contact was sound.
One of my better punches, if I do say so myself. I felt the
heavy contact of knuckle on bone and knew that it was a
good one. His eyes closed and his face shuddered. He
was out before he fell. His body tumbled heavily to the
right towards the beer-splashed floor. His beer glass spun
from his hand and, almost in slow motion, spun in the air
spewing beer in all directions. My right foot met his head
before it hit the floor, taking his front teeth out. I kicked
him so hard that it hurt my foot. Blood splattered all over
my lovely Fila trainers and socks. His face splashed against

the floor emitting a low hollow thud that made my stomach turn. A collective 'OOOO!' came from the bar full of customers. As he lay motionless at my feet, beer and blood running in a river around his head and seeping into his silver tracksuit top like an explosion transfer, I brought the heel of my right foot heavily down on his face and let out a blood-curdling 'KIAAA!' I hated doing this, but knew I had to. It was survival. If this bastard got up I could lose, and that frightened me.

Scotch jumped on my back to save his mate from any more punishment, so I threw him off and buried a left roundhouse into his belly, only slightly catching him as he scuttled out of the way.

I chased him around the bar to no avail. I looked back at Mr R; he was beginning to stir.

BANG!

Another kick that splattered into his already smashed face sent him back to sleep.

The 'haggis' was on my back again like the proverbial haversack. Again I threw him off and chased him away. He stopped at the bar, covering his unconscious mate from my punishing feet.

'What's your name?' he shouted, implying that he wanted to know the name so that, at a later date, he could 'get me sorted'.

'Geoff Thompson,' I shouted back. On hearing my name he tried to smash the plastic 'Carling Black Label' sign off the bar to use as a weapon against me, but he couldn't break it. He obviously didn't drink Carling Black Label. He opted for the weapon given to everyone who enters a public house, a beer glass. He smashed it off the bar, splinters detonating in every direction like little glass spears. He pointed its jagged edges menacingly in my direction.

The crowds of people in the pub had long since fallen deathly silent. The D.J. had stopped playing the music. A huge circle had formed to give us a fighting ground. Mr R still lay unconscious on the cold and unfriendly floor of defeat, blood oozing from his face. Gasps left many mouths as the glass shattered on the bar.

What to do, what to do? I didn't like the look of the glass and certainly didn't want to be wearing it.

I coolly picked up a pint glass from one of the many abandoned tables and emptied its contents on to the carpet then casually smashed it off the nearest table. I walked towards my Scotch friend. The look in his eyes said, 'beam me up Scottie', and I guessed he'd only broken the glass as a defensive measure. But all the same, he had broken it. We faced off taking each other's measure. 'So,' I thought, 'it's a glass fight you want, is it?'

In the mayhem Willmot-Brown had come down the stairs and witnessed the fight. He ran out of the front doors to look for Craig and John, wondering why they weren't in there already.

'CRAIG! JOHN! QUICK! INSIDE, GEOFF'S FIGHTING. QUICK! COME ON!'

CRASH!

The double front doors of the pub burst open. Craig and John burst in wielding baseball bats.

I threw my glass on the floor.

They say you can smell fear. Of course you can, especially when your opponent shits himself.

'PUT THE FUCKING GLASS DOWN!' I demanded. Scotch's eyes went from me to Craig, then from Craig to Catalogue John.

'Put your glass down or you're gonna get battered,' I told him. His eyes then fell on to the bats that the lads were wielding.

'Give me your word that my mate won't get any more,' he said.

I really admired his bottle. Faced by three men, two carrying bats, and he was prepared to get a battering to protect his mate. It would have been easy here to dish out some serious pain, but I respected his courage.

'You've got my word.'

His eyes never left Craig and John. He extended his hand toward me.

'Give me your hand.'

I took the hand and shook it.

'You've got my word.'

He immediately released his weapon.

'Nobody touch him,' I shouted to the doormen. At this, the now harmless Scotch and myself carried the unconscious and front toothless Mr R off the premises. Every voice in the room chattered excitedly. The D.J. put on another record. Civility was restored.

As Mr R's heavy body fell on to the tarmac outside the pub, I told Scotch:

'When he comes around, tell him I'll meet him any time, any place if he wants to 'go' again.'

Shortly afterwards I was reliably informed that the pair battered a taxi driver who refused to 'taxi' them.

Willmot was over the moon, he slipped me a monkey for my troubles.

'There's no need Bill, I didn't do it for the money.'

He winked and tucked the cash tightly into my hand. 'Job done, job done, it's nice to be nice, as you do, as you do.'

I laughed and took the money.

This situation is still in the air (at the time of first writing, 1993). Scotch has sent down several messages apologising profusely for his behaviour. I admired him greatly for backing his mate on the night, he's a very brave man. I just can't understand what he's doing knocking around with a waster like Mr R. Mr R has sent down several messages saying he's going to shoot me. I, as a bit of insurance, obtained his home address, as I always do with people who cross swords with me; just in case!

A week later the threats are lessening and the stress aftermath has almost lost its impetus. Life is again returning to normal, though of course, I'm still on my guard. I'm always on my guard.

5. Money for Old Rope

Colin was an amiable enough chap of about twenty, five foot eight and thin, with long, black, curly hair and a gaunt face. Not the most intelligent of people but not stupid either. He lived at home with his mum and step-dad and worked by day in a Rugby garage owned by P. When he wasn't working, he spent most of his time and money in the Crow public house on the Bolton Road, where he was a popular regular. Life was sweet, until Colin's boss P gave him the sack for reasons unknown. In a small one horse town like Rugby, jobs were hard to come by so Colin was understandably devastated.

One night, after an evening in the Crow he decided to get revenge on his former boss by hitting him where it really hurt, in his Rolls-Royce. Colin knew that the car was his boss' absolute pride and joy and that any damage he could do to the said vehicle would be as good as kicking the man straight in the bollocks (which he'd like to do as well, but never had the guts). His first tactical error was telling one or two of his buddies in the Crow, as you do when you've just swallowed seven pints of lager, of his intentions.

'If 'e thinks 'e can just get rid of me and that's the end of it, 'e's got another thought coming.'

Almost immediately after emptying a two-pound bag of sugar into the petrol tank of the Roller, and completely fucking up the engine, everyone in the sparsely-populated neighbourhood, where even flatulence made the news headlines, knew who and why, and probably even where he brought the sugar. This was by far his biggest mistake, a mistake that would alter the course of his young life – drastically.

Six thousand pounds worth of repairs later, P was more than a little perturbed and absolutely had to get his revenge. He didn't want to involve the police because all that meant was months of waiting for a court date and years of waiting for compensation from a numbingly slow judicial system. And then there was his credibility. How could he retain his image as a hard man if he involved the police? He fancied himself as the toughest man in Rugby, which in real terms is like being the toughest man in your street. No, better to do it like they do in the films and put a contract out on Colin. That way he would get his revenge and not only retain his image but probably even heighten it. Yes, no one would fuck with him after that.

He knew a few doormen in neighbouring Coventry, where 'mad bastards' were in abundance; they'd sort it out for him.

A phone call to L with the offer of £1,000 for a good job well done, and it was sorted.

'Of course I want the money back L, but I also want you to teach this boy a lesson, he needs to know that I'm not a man to be messed with, you know what I'm saying, don't you?'

'Oh yeah P, it's not a problem, I'll get the lads to sort it.'

L was a thick-set, forty-eight-year-old with greying hair, a generous nose, and a constant, irritating fidget, like he was permanently waiting for a late bus. He ran a Coventry door agency and held many contacts.

A chain of phone calls was made. L rang M, a huge man with digger bucket hands and a face that'd scare your kids. He rang his brother-in-law S, who in return, rang D.

Together, and for a guaranteed £250-a-piece, a good job was ensured. After all, they worked the door and gave out 'slaps' frequently anyway; £250 was just icing on the cake.

After a brief conversation and absolutely no planning the lads decided to go over to Rugby to check out the target and eye-up the territory. M drove, S and D sat in the passenger and rear seats respectively. L stayed at home, his end of the deal was already completed. He was no mug, he was being paid for organising the job, you could do that on the phone, and there was no need to take any risks.

D, from Willenhall, was the black sheep of his family and was well akin to violence. He'd worked on any door that would pay him, fighting with any man who dared cross him. His blond handlebar moustache bristled under a pug nose, and small light blue eyes glared out from beneath a hat of blond hair. Hugely built at seventeen stone, he looked like cardboard cutout of Hulk Hogan. S sat behind him, so big at six foot five and nineteen stone that he had to duck his head under the roof of the Cortina. He had an infectious laugh and a sharp wit, and with a couple of neck bolts, S could have doubled for Herman Munster.

The car groaned under the combined weight of fifty-two stone as it chugged towards Rugby.

Up the busy Binley Road, on to Brandon Road, passing the tranquil Wolston and the countrified Long Lawford. Then into quiet Rugby to the popular Crow public house, which sat regally at the top of six steps, with a lounge to the left, a bar to the right and a lovely garden at the rear. Understandably, many eyes glanced up as they entered the plush lounge of the pub. Each of the three looked like heavies from a sixties gangster movie. Colin was quickly spotted from a small photo M had been given. M, in his wisdom, decided to approach Colin and have a quiet word in his ear. D and S stood back so as not to look too ominous – a difficult task.

There was a tension in the air that D and S knew well, it was neither welcomed nor shunned, it was just the expected introduction to violence. To the locals it was as welcome as a hedgehog shit, an unwelcome addition to their Sunday afternoon drinking session.

Unbeknown to D and S, M made a little deal with Colin.

'Colin,' (M tried to mimic affection, but that's not easy when you've got a voice with muscles) 'you know the crack, you know why we're here, we're getting good money to break something but it doesn't have to be like that. We could sort it out.' Colin nodded his mouth slightly ajar like a dumbstruck schoolboy. 'Can you sort out the money for the Roller by next week?'

'Er, yeah, I fink so.' Of course he knew he couldn't but he wasn't going to tell that to these monsters.

M felt pleased with himself, for all his size and experience with violence he was basically a good man. If he could 'sort' this fellow without pain he would. He patted Colin on the shoulder.

'Good man. I'll tell you what to do, hang a sling around your shoulder and we'll tell the man that we've done a job on ya' OK?' Colin nodded. 'Then give me a ring next week, when you've got P's money for the car repairs, and no one will be any the wiser.' M gave him a knowing wink. 'I'll even slip you a ton for your troubles.' This brought a smile to Colin's face.

Both were delighted with the deal. They parted company, Colin promised to get the money and M gave him a contact number to ring when he had.

In the car on the way back to Coventry when the lads were talking about what had been said in the pub, M never told them about his 'little deal'.

'So wot's the score?' asked D in a naturally gruff voice.

'Yeah, wot 'd' 'ave to say for himself, did you tell 'im wot 'e wus gonna get if 'e don't get the money?' added S.

'Don't worry, don't worry, he knows the score, I've given him to next Sunday to sort it. He's fucking shitting bowling balls, he's not gonna fuck.'

'I 'ope 'e doesn't for 'is sake, weedy little bastud, 'e was a right streak of piss; if you 'ad 'ave spit on 'im 'e'd 'ave strangled.'

S and D laughed.

'I can't see any of the locals getting involved if we do 'ave to sort 'im, they were a right load of country bumpkins.'

By the following Sunday Colin hadn't rung. M contacted S and D, his plan hadn't worked.

'He's gonna have to have a slap,' he told D on the phone. 'Little wanker, I was really nice to 'im as well.'

''Ow ya gonna work it then?'

'We'll give him a little bit of a slap, then give him another couple of days to get the money together. We'll have to give him some pain though or he won't take it serious.'

'Who's gonna do it, me 'n' S?

'Yeah, I think so, I'll drive the car. It won't take much whoever does it, you'd have more trouble fighting the current when in the bath.'

'I'll bring some thin' wi' me, just in case.'

M rang L.

'What do you think, do you want us to give 'im some?' Even over the phone M could sense L fidgeting around like a tramp's vest.

'Oh yeah, he'll have to have it, that's what the man says, I don't think he ever really expects to see the money, he just wants to make an example.'

Between them they decided to do it straight away, to get it over and done with.

That night, Sunday at eight p.m., for the second time they drove through the sleepy countryside that lay between Coventry and Rugby to do the dirty deed. D was armed with a twelve inch long piece of lead-filled conduit pipe.

The warm evening sun beat down on the slightly battered blue S-reg. Cortina. D and S, who were, to be honest, pissed, laughed and joked, all the way to the Crow. They thought little of the task that lay ahead, only that a cheeky, young, local lad was going to get a slap, nothing more than that. And they would all be £250 heavier in the hip pocket for it. None thought about the seriousness of the matter, nor the dire consequences that might follow. None thought about whether they might get caught. They all just thought it was a bit of a wheeze, if they did get caught they'd only get a slap on the wrist at the very most.

D and S stretched their cramped muscles as they emerged from the car. M stayed in the driver's seat as getaway man.

Once out of the car and stretched, D and S's moods changed, and they got themselves into fight-mode. The clowning duo transformed themselves into 'heavies'; they looked mean and ugly. 'I'll do it, you watch my back, all right?' D was very matter of fact, S nodded his assent.

'I'm not gonna fuck around, just in, give it 'im and away, anyone gets in my way you 'fuck' them.' S nodded again. The time for talk was over. They pounded into the pub.

The July sun shone down on the Crow public house. Inside, gossiping banter quizzed across table tops and 'Lassie' dogs sat obediently at their masters' feet. The portly, red-faced landlord stood sentry-like at the end of the bar drinking away profits and heading for a heart attack, leaving his spot very occasionally, and only then to pinch the barmaid's ample bottom. Local farmers with a taste for beer and a distaste for strangers sat at pine tables talking about how they 'can't read and can't write, but cun druyve a track-urr'. Would-be darts pros with 'Jockey Wilson' bellies and plastic flight darts hitting the board in all the wrong places dreamed of one day playing the circuit. A fat lady with 'wide load' knickers and an even fatter laugh solemnly tells her companions that she 'hardly eats a thing' and 'everything I do eat just turns to fat'. Colin, dressed like a scarecrow in *Worzel Gummage* hand-me-downs, sat quietly with his father-in-law at a table close to the bar. He was sipping his usual half, because 'I can't really afford to drink now that I haven't got a job'. He was blissfully unaware of how close the mantle of retribution lay, and that he wouldn't be enjoying his half for much longer.

The lads entered the busy bar, D with the conduit pipe tucked into his grey leather jacket. He felt good now, and so did S. Again, all eyes were on them as they entered but this just blew their egos even bigger. Colin's father-in-law was a big, barrel-chested man of about forty with thinning hair, and a red, veined face that looked like a map of Europe. His eyes were of a bloodshot hue. S approached the hapless Colin through the crowd of people. D followed, stopping a short distance back.

Smoke herded the air. The smell of country wafted in in warm waves. Whispers broke out through the room like a conspiracy, a hundred voices fusing into one inaudible hum. All eyes universally followed the two strangers. They stood out like a eunuch on a nudist beach.

D and S both breathed in deeply to control the flow; they were 'in mode'. The fight was on.

'Can I have a little word with you outside?' S asked evenly.

Colin, who must have thought 'a word' really did mean 'a word' and not a battering, agreed effusively. But as he stood up to leave his father-in-law grabbed him by the arm and pulled him back.

'He's going nowhere,' he said, staring at S and D defiantly. 'Anything you've got to say to 'im can be said here.'

Colin's eyes darted pathetically from the lads to his father-in-law, and then back again, almost apologetically. For a moment there was a deathly silence, the room muted in anticipation. This was a complication that S and D hadn't counted for, actually they hadn't counted for anything other than a compliant victim.

D and the father-in-law eyed each other like latter-day cowboys. The tension was palpable. The locals held their breath. This was more exciting than *Emmerdale Farm*.

D slowly pulled the lead pipe from his jacket
'Is that right?' There was menace in D's voice.

M, outside in the getaway car was starting to get a little
restless. He stood out here like a bulldog's bollocks. He
was starting to regret the whole issue. It felt wrong, they'd
not planned a single thing, save the fact that D was going
to bash Colin on the head with the pipe. No strategies, no
false number plates (or better still a stolen car), no alibis
should it all go wrong, nothing. As he sat in the car he
realised what a balls-up this could be should complications
arise. They'd only been in there a couple of minutes but it
seemed like an hour. Everyone who walked past the car
looked in at him. He looked like he was on a 'hit'. 'Where
the fuck are they?' he whispered to himself.

BANG!

D whacked the pipe straight across the crown of Colin's
head, bursting his skull into a gaping crimson vein of
blood. His body spiralled and he fell face-first, heavy and
lifeless, on to and through a table full of drinks. He was
unconscious. For a split-second no one moved as though
frozen in time, then, as one, the whole pub exploded.
The father-in-law lunged angrily at D, only to be coshed
just as quickly, and just as savagely. He crashed to the
floor at D's feet, just holding on to consciousness, grabbing
hold of D's legs in a frantic attempt at keeping him in the
pub, and in the hope that it might curb the 'caning' he
was about to get.

As D battered him with the pipe again and again, a
huge virago of a woman, who must have topped the scales

at twenty stone, jumped on S's back, biting, scratching and pinching him. D was still whacking the father-in-law, so much so that he lost control of the pipe and it disappeared under dozens of feet. As he smashed the father-in-law's face through the glass patio doors in a last-ditch attempt at releasing the leech, more attacking bodies flailed in at him, so he counter-lashed in every direction – if it moved he hit it. As S spun around trying to get the 'fat piece' off his back, her chubby face came into view for a millisecond, so he punched her hard in the eye. She squealed and held the eye in an attempt at assuaging the pain, giving S a chance of breaking free. She shouldn't have been 'hanging around' strange men anyway. Together they fought their way through the door and back on to the street and ran for the cramped sanctuary of the waiting Cortina.

M started the engine up ready to go, but before the lads reached the car D stopped dead in his tracks. 'Oh fuck!' he screamed.

'What?' shouted S.

'I've left the fucking pipe in the pub, it'll have my 'prints all over it. We'll have to go back in.'

S closed his eyes and shook his head in disgust.

'You stupid bastard, how could you do this to me?'

Without demur, D and S ran back into the pub to retrieve 'the evidence'. As soon as the locals saw the pair the battle started again; punches, kicks, bites, butts and spits filled the scene as D and S fought their way back to get the pipe. Amazingly, D found it lying in a corner of the room by the smashed bloodstained patio doors. Quickly – amid much violence, mayhem, smashed glass, spilt beer, toppled tables, shouts, screams, grunts and groans – they ran kicking, punching and 'piping' back through the crowds and out to the waiting car, where an impatient M whisked them off to comparatively quiet Coventry.

All the way home, S and D laughed till their eyes smarted with tears and their stomachs cramped with the effort. Their laughter was to be short-lived.

The Crow public house had never seen such devastation and, although all had risen admirably and stoically to the occasion, they were now suffused with a cocktail of feelings: anger, fear and confusion – fear rising above the rest. In an instant their lives were upside down. All of a sudden that overdue phone bill, leaking roof or marital argument seemed insignificant by comparison. This kind of violence was way beyond them. Every blow, scream, spill of blood and smash of glass would be etched into their minds for ever more, bringing serenity closer for some, heart attacks and ulcers closer for others. Rising to violence on the spur and fighting without the common sense of thought as an interfering factor is very easy because it is instinctive. It goes way back to primeval days where mankind had to fight to survive and violence was as natural as eating and drinking. The aftermath of fear and stress are not so easy to control though, and make people's lives a misery.

Pedantic yet happy life in the Crow had changed immeasurably in the space of only minutes; mayhem had reared its ugly head and roared into their lives like a hurricane.

Colin still lay motionless amid the disarray of broken glass, spilled beer and upturned tables, deep in the arms of unconsciousness. His already-pale hue was paler from the beating.

The fat lady, taking up three chairs and a small table (perhaps this thing wouldn't be over until she sang) cried uncontrollably and nursed her swelling black eye, which looked comically absurd on such an obese face, like a cartoon shiner. The father-in-law, with a face of bloody melancholy, held a handkerchief to his head to stem the blood, and shook with embarrassment.

'Bastards,' he said every few seconds.

People surrounded each victim, praising and sympathising in an attempt at mollifying their sorrow and pain. A fetid stench wafted around the room. Colin's bowels had emptied themselves. A large dark and wet stain spread around the crotch of his navy trousers.

The ambulance was on its way. Colin's breathing was shallow and erratic; he looked on the verge of death.

To D and S, fighting was a common occurrence. Most weekends would see them in the thick of battle in one pub or another. They'd grown to expect it, even to like it. Both knew it was wrong but neither could, or for that matter would, pull themselves away. They knew that the violence and fighting was wrong, but the cash and local fame made it more than worthwhile. They liked being 'someone'. In their own environment they were stars.

Bouncing, D had surmised, might well be a mug's game, but he was the best-dressed, best-treated, most respected mug he'd ever known.

D had a good steady job in the day at the Jaguar car plant, moving bits and pieces around all day on the forklift truck.

'The Door', though, was beginning to envelope him, taking over his life. He'd started doing the odd night here and there for a bit of pocket money, not realising it would suck him in like a whirlpool and not let him go. Before he knew it, he was working every night and in charge of several teams, answering only to L, who paid him handsomely for his trouble.

He enjoyed his work so much that he was seriously thinking about giving up his day job for it. Many before him had done so and regretted it.

The life of a doorman is, or can be, short-lived. After a few years of it, or maybe just a few months, when the novelty wears off, he'll be praying for a straight job, praying for a life without violence and its ugly handmaiden, stress. Praying also for a quiet night at home with the wife and kids. Praying for a life.

When the phone rang in the front room of D's smart, well furnished Binley house, he picked it up without hesitation. Later, when stress and fear are on the agenda, he'd learn to hate the phone, its ring becoming synonymous with bad news and trouble. Thursday night, six thirty p.m. almost time for his last night-shift of that week.

'D,' said the shaky, disembodied voice on the other end of the line. It was S's sister, who was married to M, the getaway driver. 'The police have been around looking for M.'

D didn't answer. He felt his bowels twitch uncomfortably and his mind buzz with a paroxysm of thoughts.

Sun Tzu said that those who wish to 'wage war' should first count the cost. Aftermath had arrived. The second fight, the real fight, had just begun.

M and S worked together in the family business, 'Neat Sheet Metal Co.' (for want of a better alias). M was oblivious at that time to the police visit, he was happy and content. Last weekend was already lost in his memory. It was just another situation that had come and gone. They hadn't been paid for it yet, either.

The small factory unit lay neatly within a family of units, recently built on the clean Alderman's Green industrial estate, that lay precariously between Potters Green, cosy Alderman's Green, and Woodend. When M saw the police car pull slowly into his works car park, he felt all the same feelings that D had done, only worse; after all it was his phone number that 'Unconscious Colin' was holding. Something he'd neglected to tell the lads and something he hoped – prayed – would not come to light, though deep down he knew it eventually would. He quickly ran into the small factory office to S.

'Quick, fuck off out the back, the Law's here.' He shooed him urgently with his hands as he spoke.

When S saw the panda car through the office window he disappeared out of the factory, and made his way straight down to the pub. A couple of pints would definitely, he assured himself, help to put things a little into perspective. If not, a few more would help put him into an uncaring, burping, farting heap.

M was taken straight to the station for questioning.

At the other end of the city, D sat alone with loneliness in a rough Willenhall bar where the locals picked their teeth with Catnaps, and shotguns were as perfunctory as the tables and chairs. He was comfortable here; these were his kind of people. He was searching for what S had already found . . . oblivion.

Within an hour of the police arresting M, they were on D and S's tracks. They knew everything, even before they had picked up any of the lads. There were so many witnesses that the case was already watertight, still, it wouldn't hurt to get confessions as well.

M had vowed not to open his mouth, promised for his and the lads' sakes not to say anything, he could handle it, he knew he could. But as soon as C.I.D. got him alone, they knew they could trick him. They'd seen it all. People who were tough and people who only thought they were, those who knew the crack, and others who didn't have a fucking clue. M was tough, but he hadn't any idea about police procedure, the games that they play and the little white lies they tell to get you to talk.

The D.C. in charge at Ryton was a hard-eyed, gum-chewing, smart soldier-like character, with an air of arrogance that came with his badge. He couldn't believe his luck. Every trick he'd tried on M had worked, starting straight away with the 'you do realise the seriousness of this charge, don't you?' ploy, which shook M to his boots. After telling M how much trouble he was in and that he could be looking at a charge of attempted murder they left him in an empty cell with nothing but rogue thoughts. They knew that his own mind would do most of the work for them, spiraling him down into ever-increasing misery until he would snatch desperately at any offer they made him.

After an hour, M was, to say the least, perturbed but still holding on. He'd managed to deny everything until D.C. Bustard played out his ace card, shooting M down in flames.

'I'm telling you now that if you don't start getting a little more co-operative,' he emphasised the word 'co-operative', 'you're gonna have the whole fucking lot. We don't really give a monkey's fuck whether we get the others or not, so long as we've got you. Think about it, you're already looking at attempted murder, if you don't tell us your part in it we're gonna add blackmail and extortion.' M's eyes shot forward in surprise. 'You're gonna be looking at some serious time.' He'd got M on the run, and he paused deliberately to let the seriousness of the words sink in, then continued. 'Look at the fucking size of you man, what jury in the world is going to believe it wasn't you? You could be a fucking priest looking like that and they'd still send you down the steps. So do yourself a big favour and give us what we want, it'll save a lot of fucking around in the long run.'

The words sliced him to pieces, cut his will to the bone, crushed it flatter than paper. He thought that perhaps the police were bluffing, but he couldn't take the chance. What about the lads though? He couldn't give them up, but if he didn't his family would be taken away from him. The D.C. threw a pile of witness statements on the table in front of him.

'We've got you anyway M, it'll make it easier on you and the lads if you give us a full confession.'

M thought for a long moment, shook his head in the hope that perhaps it was all a bad dream, but his face held a look of defeat.

A short time later S was arrested at home. D, on hearing of the two arrests, went on another mad drinking spree instead of going to work that night. After all, if he was caught and remanded in custody, who knows when he might get another chance.

D's slim blonde wife lay with her head on his chest in the darkened bedroom of their house. Twelve thirty in the morning and they still weren't asleep.

'What's going to happen D, will it mean prison?'

D was quiet for a moment. 'Naw,' he tried to console her, 'we'll get off with a warnin', no one ever gets bird first time around, anyway, there's hardly any room in the jails so they're giving out loads of community hours. You just look sad in the courts, tell 'im you're sorry and 'e'll give ya loads of old ladies' gardens to dig.'

Neither believed it.

That night, despite having a good drink in him, D tossed and turned, not even finding a sanctuary in his own bed. There's no hiding place from stress, you have to just stand and fight . . . or fall.

D spent the next couple of days slipping the rapidly closing police net. Through the grapevine, he was told by the coppers to: 'Give yourself up, or it'll be worse for you when we do get you.'

Bowing to the inevitable, D did give himself up.

As the panda drove D over to Rugby police station he felt relief that it was over and that he'd been 'nabbed'.

'You do realise,' said D.C. Bustard, relishing in D's plight, 'that you could be charged with attempted murder.' This part-truth, part-ploy left D's temporary relief in a sorry state of decimation. As his face flushed red, his bottom spewed out a blast of wind that choked the car like C.S. gas. Even the noxious smell of D's unloaded anal passage didn't wipe the smile off the face of D.C. Bustard, who'd never enjoyed so much success. He mentally rubbed his hands together with glee.

Initially, S and D, both knowing the crack, denied everything and pleaded not guilty to all charges, until, that is, they were shown the overwhelming evidence against them. M's statement, the phone number from Colin, witness statements from the Crow, and a witness outside the pub who had jotted down their number plate.

The game was up.

D admitted his part in it and was charged with section 18: wounding with intent, eventually getting it dropped to the lesser, though still serious, section 20: wounding.

S still denied his part in it all, despite everything else. This denial was agitating the police no end, after all, everyone else was playing the game, so why shouldn't S? He needed a little friendly persuasion. D.C. Bustard was pretty good at 'friendly persuasion'.

'Plead to section 20,' he told S, 'or we're going to charge you with attempted murder, blackmail and demanding money with menaces.'

By comparison, S thought section 20 looked pretty damned good, so snapped up the D.C.'s offer.

By January of the next year, the lads had been to court six times, each time with adjournment due to social reports, etc.

Late January saw them in Crown Court under the judgeship of one of the county's most formidable judges, famous around these parts for his harsh sentences and hatred of criminals. Obviously they were guilty before they even started on account of the fact that they'd pleaded guilty, so it was just a case of sentencing. S, D and M (L & P never got roped in), were all pretty sure that they would get away with a severe reprimand, commonly known as a 'slapped wrist'. The judge didn't see it quite like that. In summing up at the end of the trial he said:

'This is the worst case of unprovoked violence I've ever witnessed, relating back to the blackmailing, racketeering gangsters of the sixties. I shall, very reluctantly, grant you bail whilst we await social reports, but I warn you now, prepare yourself for a custodial sentence.'

3rd March 1989 – the lads, dressed in their best 'court suits', stood in the dock to await sentence. They all still hoped to escape a jail term, but realistically they knew that 'they never had a chance'. Their sentences were announced.

S, thirty months in prison.

D, thirty months in prison.

M, thirty months in prison.

S thanked the judge effusively. D and M bowed their heads low as they were all led 'down the steps'.

'Brilliant, great,' said a rejoicing S as they were led to a cell underneath the courts. 'We'll be out in six weeks.'

D lifted his head up, and looked at S, bemused.

'Six weeks? 'Ow the fuck do you work that out?'

'Well,' began S, smiling broadly, 'three months sentence, with good behaviour, and we'll be out in six weeks.'

D shook his head.

'*Thirty* months, you stupid cunt, not three.'

S's lower lip hit the floor in disbelief and his legs wobbled; he felt faint. D was a buttock-clenching millisecond away from soiling his undergarments. M's whole body shook; he thought he'd died and gone to hell. In the cell awaiting transport to Winston Green, they sang 'We're All Going on a Summer Holiday'.

Thirty months was the prison sentence they received.

D also lost his job, his car, his liberty and two precious years out of his children's lives.

M lost his business, his credibility, his dignity, his liberty and also two years out of his children's lives.

S lost his business, his flat, his car and his liberty.

'Unconscious Colin' never recovered fully from his head wound and now walks around in a drunken stupor, slurring his words and seemingly oblivious to anything surrounding him. He'll never work again.

All this and no money ever changed hands.

6. 'Pigs' in the Middle

Pretty girls at an 'acid party' are always in abundance. On this warm July night it was altogether too much for me and my little mate 'downstairs' (my willy). To take my mind off the frustrating arousal and the terrible din these people called music, I let my mind wander back three hours to Nobby's place where I sat with a half of lager and a bag of smoky bacon crisps waiting for my lift. They were late. They said they'd be here by midnight but it was now twelve thirty a.m. I wanted to go home, oh how I wanted to go home. But the hundred quid I was promised for working the Hinckley acid party was too much to turn down. All the same, if they didn't come for me soon I was going home. A warm bed seemed more attractive right now than a ton in the back pocket. The headlights of the red Nissan Bluebird estate flashed three times through the back entrance window of Nobby's. A lead weight pulled down at my heart and I heaved a heavy, tired, pissed off sigh, 'oh shit'. The bubble of a warm bed burst and I was on my way.

We left the city centre and before my sleepy eyes knew it we were on the M69 towards Leicester. The car was filled with a mixture of doormen and punters. Gaz, a short, stocky, moustached friend of mine drove. Everyone in the car was talking but it all sounded garbled because I was too tired to be interested. I lifted my bottom off the seat to release my sweat-sticky trousers from my legs. A black guy next to me with half-closed eyes lit up a spliff and drew heavily upon it, held the smoke in his mouth momentarily then billowed it out like furnace fumes, filling the car. This brought a whole new meaning to the words

'passive smoking'. I felt my frowning mouth lift
involuntarily into a grin and as my eyes widened and my
heart began to jump and dance under my shirt. I
instinctively breathed in deeply through my nose and my
fingers tapped my legs merrily to the beat of the music
that a moment ago didn't seem to exist.

'Yes, yes, yes,' I thought, 'I can't wait to get there.'

The house was big, but just a dot in the middle of the
acres of countryside that surrounded it. The nearest
neighbour was at least a mile away. The country lane the
house sat on was wide enough for only one vehicle at a
time. Cars were parked as far as the eye could see; on the
grass and in the ditches all the way down the lane. The
house was white and huge with a high-tiled roof, and it
boasted a half-acre garden, every inch of which was
covered by bopping, bouncing bodies. From the sky it
must have looked like an army of ants around a sugar
lump.

The monotonous, meaningless music attacked my ears
and I wondered if this was hell. Ten of us were guarding,
six with Alsatian dogs. The eleventh was given his
marching orders because his dog bit Tony 'the Head' on
the ankle with absolutely no provocation. Four of us were
veteran doormen, the dog handlers, though, were just your
run-of-the-mill security. They would have served only as
cannon-fodder if it 'kicked off'.

I watched as two beautiful ladies paid their entrance to
the party. One was tall with mousy-brown hair, big eyes,
lovely pouting lips and a body that would have awoken
the beast in a priest. She was gorgeous, from the little
high vest that tantalisingly bared her mid-riff, down to
the black trousers that hugged her bottom tightly at the

top before splaying out into bagginess at the leg. Her mate was blonde and just as pretty, slightly shorter but still tall. Her blouse was ghostly transparent just how I like them. It only just covered her internal organs. I like that in a dress. Her short skirt was figure-hugging and did very little to hide her lovely white pants underneath.

They walked on to the grass dance floor with confidence. At that point no one knew that they were off-duty policewomen.

Personally I'm very pro-police. I think they do a hard and thankless job, but my views were shared by none of the clientele at this rave. It was a mugger's mall, a crook's convention and a fighter's feast. There were some heavy, heavy people around who did not like the intrusion of the Law, even if 'it' was off-duty. They stood out like a bloody nose at a baptism. When you've dealt with the Law or have been dealt with by the Law, you learn to sense it, smell it, even taste it. These two beautiful girls who were, quite honestly, only out for a good night, were spotted in seconds. The arm of the Law might well be long, but it wouldn't stretch to the aid of these two tonight.

I watched with growing concern as a ring of taunting youths encircled them. I eyed their faces as the beauty faded to pale.

The organisers of the rave, who were also, as coincidence would have it, the leaders of the infamous Bell Green crew broke the circle and approached the girls menacingly.

'Wot's the crack? Wot the fuck are ya doin' 'ere? Spying, ya fucking spying are ya? You're Law, I can smell you from 'ere.'

The man with the questions was tall and ginger with a hard face; a model for 'wanted' posters, you know the type.

The girls were frightened, they were only out for a good night, the last thing they wanted was trouble, especially right out in the middle of nowhere.

'No,' said the blonde, we're just out for a good night, that's all.'

'You're filth though, ain't ya?'

The dark-haired girl spoke up. 'We are in the police, but that's not why we're here, we just thought . . .' Ginger interrupted.

'Ya never thought fucking nothin', we don't want you 'ere, you're scum.'

The blonde went for the obvious, 'Let us go then, we don't want any trouble, just let us go home.'

'Oh yeah? So you can ring your mates to come and close us down? You can stay 'ere for the rest of the night, where we can keep an eye on ya.'

The girls looked at each other in dismay. For the rest of the night this was to be their prison. They couldn't leave until the next day and even then not until the very last person had left the party. All the security were told that if they tried to leave they were to be hurt. If they let them go now they would surely inform their colleagues of the whereabouts of this illegal rave.

'Let's just batter them and fuck them out into a field' was one of the many suggestions. Many other threats and insults were maliciously tossed at the girls. I still watched from a short distance away. The taller of the two looked particularly frightened, the other didn't look too happy either.

Nev, the leader of the Bell Green crew, stood tall, lean and meticulously smart, from his one hundred pound Torsion trainers through his Pepe jeans to his Tachini top, even to the short side-parted soldier-smart cut of his hair. His nose had a central break in it from one of his many pro-boxing bouts, but it only served to fine tune his character. Big in fashion he may have been, big in heart he definitely wasn't.

Expressionlessly he listened to the girls pleading for their freedom. Their promise of secrecy hit a blank wall.

'Just let us go, we promise that we won't say anything, honest.'

'NO,' Nev underlined, 'you stay here all night, it's as much as I can do to stop these people fucking you up, now keep out of my face.'

I speculated that they might cry, and if they thought it would have helped I think they would have done, but it wouldn't, so they didn't.

The sound of a taxi pulling up outside the gates of the house distracted me. More partygoers hitting for a high slithered out of the black cab doors laughing and joking and completely unperturbed by the twenty-five pound entrance fee. Spotlights above the rave entrance shadowed the guards and their dogs and reflected off the roof of the purring cab.

I approached it, pushing my way through the hundreds of revellers, young and old, though mostly young, walking through the guard. I poked my head through the side window of the taxi. The driver thought this amusing because he hadn't wound the window down.

'Hang on a minute,' I said to the flat-capped cabby, 'I've got someone to go back.' He nodded his appreciation;

another thirty quid. I walked back through the guards, through the punters, through the music and through the mayhem and stood in front of the girls in blue. They stared at me in unison, looking deep into my eyes, desperately seeking a friend. I held both my hands out towards them offering a lifeline. They took a hand each, and everybody stared and whispered and pointed as I turned and walked hand-in-hand with these two beautiful frightened ladies, back through the mayhem, the music, the punters, then the guards who looked at each other in astonishment. I felt good as they released their tight grip on my hands to get into the cab.

Revellers surrounded the cab so it couldn't move off straight away, and the girls looked scared. At that moment a panda car pulled up and Nev walked over to talk to them. The girls watched out of the taxi window. The moment was tense. I thought they might call out to the police in the panda, but they did the exact opposite, they slid down on the seats and tried to hide. It was obvious that they didn't want to be seen.

After a long minute the panda drove off, followed shortly after by the cab.

There was not a word spoken but the thanks was in their eyes as the taxi whisked them away.

I walked back through the guards. No one approached me, and nobody spoke. This was respect.

7. Main en Main

To my mind, the ultimate act of courage is to fight one-to-one, or *main en main*, as the French might say. Why? Because to fight alone takes ultimate courage and self-control. The only fire-power you carry is that which lies within you. It doesn't matter who you know, who your 'back-up' is or even how many Dans you hold – or even if you are Desperate Dan – because none of it counts when a 'straightener' is arranged. All your allies just step back and leave you to it, and if you haven't got it, the 'belt' will do nothing more than make you look a bigger twat when you lose.

'One-on-ones' always sort the men out from the boys. The majority of fighters won't (or at least their bottle won't) stretch beyond gang fighting where they are lost in the crowd, and single-minded courage isn't needed or called upon quite so much.

To stand alone with only the crutch of your own courage is the ultimate expression of bravery. I've seen fewer braver – and even fewer I admire more – than a school friend of mine, many years ago at Cardinal Wiseman Boys' school, which held lessons for hundreds of working class Catholic boys around the city.

Every class in every school has its 'swots': Wiseman was no exception to this rule.

As a kid I sat precariously on the fence between being a swot and being one of the boys, never quite making up my mind which side of the enclosure I wanted to be on. I longed to be one of the 'boys', and tried to with my Doctor Martin boots, stay-press trousers and cool

Barathea jacket that hung from my skinny frame like a Big Daddy overcoat; but, at the same time I enjoyed a rapport with the teachers' pets. My baby face and the dead give-away, the briefcase, clashed terribly with the 'hard man' clothing, giving me a look of a social schizophrenic. In my latter years at school, when my own bullies were tossed by the wayside and courage was born from it, I became a protector for the swots, fighting off the 'boys' who always preyed upon them.

I walked then, as I do now, the fine and dangerous line between the literary and the criminally educated, gaining respect, I hope, from both quarters.

Don majored in bullying. As a bully, he was top of the class. He considered the swots as subordinates whose staid gait was like red rag to a bull. Every day would see 'Don the Menace' sweeping the playground like a tide of misery, taking money, sweets, pens, pencils and anything else that took his fancy from those weaker than himself. Swatting those who argued back like newspapered bluebottles. Built like a pitbull, only more aggressive and with a lower I.Q., Don was always fighting; whether it was on the rugger field, where even the referee gave him a wide berth, or in the boxing ring, where they nicknamed him 'Animal' because he was. Even on the dance floor at the local disco where he ruled the roost, fighting took precedence over dancing. He didn't care that he drove misery into the hearts of everyone he crossed, like a stake. He knew his strength and he thrived upon it.

Gold-rimmed spectacles sat on a small, lily-white nose that was peppered with freckles; face pinched; uniform meticulously clean down to the spit-polished shine on his shoes and neat mousy-coloured, side-parted hair. He was a prime target. He had 'victim' written all over him. Don had noticed him on more than one occasion; he was just waiting for the right moment.

After lunch break one Wednesday afternoon, Don pulled him, he was sure he could extort money or dinner tickets from this likely-looking candidate.

A hundred kids of every shape and size passed by the pair on their way to class. They stood between two school blocks. Science block to the left, English block to the right. Don poked David hard in the chest.

'Give me your money,' he demanded menacingly. David surprisingly, looked unperturbed.

I was one of the hundreds of kids crossing on my way to the English block. I stood a safe distance back and watched as David placed his brown leather briefcase on the ground beside him.

'No,' he said, without even a hint of fear in his voice. Don looked around him, not believing his own ears. He pushed David.

'What do you mean, "no"?'

'How many different connotations does the word hold? No means no, no matter how you say it,' David replied.

Don was dumbfounded, he had no conception of verbal arguments, so went for the familiar:

'If you don't give me your money, then I'm gonna hit you.'

'That'll stop him in his tracks,' he must have thought.

'All right then, hit me,' said David, calm and apparently fearless. Don's mouth gaped open in shock. This was a level he'd never had to rise to before. He felt a fear in his belly to which he wasn't familiar and he didn't like it – and what the fuck does 'connotation' mean? Don looked around him at all the people milling about. He searched desperately for a friendly face. This school didn't hold one for him. He laughed aloud dramatically to try to hide his fear. Then said – almost shouted – to no one in particular:

'He wants to fight me. Reckons he's not scared.' He looked back at David, whose eyes held a strength that unnerved him, frightened him. He felt out of his league, he didn't want to be there. In a bid to escape, Don tried to switch the onus.

'So you'll fight anyone will you?' David knew this game, so threw the onus back.

'Yes anyone, but especially you. I'm not afraid of you.'

Don's will was beaten. Another fake laugh left his lips, then he let himself get carried away in the tide of people.

'I'll see you again,' Don threatened, unconvincingly. Then disappeared on a sea of school kids into the Science block.

David didn't even celebrate with a smile. He picked up his briefcase and walked to his next lesson. He was oblivious to my admiration. In years to come when sticky situations called for inspiration to pull my courage to the forefront I would use his example.

I never remember seeing David again after that incident, though I never, ever forgot him.

Tony and Jimmy had met twice before in combat, both occasions failing to reach a conclusion, both occasions left in 'mid-air' as it were. Due to these unfinished battles, a great hate had developed between the two of them. To put the burgeoning hate to bed once and for all they arranged a 'straightener'.

Tony the Head topped the scales at a robust twenty-one stone, with several hundred previous wins behind him. He had though, in his time, been stabbed more times that a dressmaker's thumb and held many 'Mars Bars' to prove it. One razor scar went from the right side of his forehead, right through his eyebrow, and down through his cheek, where it met with a multitude of other scars, each telling its own story.

Jimmy was light at twelve stone, but punched harder than he should have done at this weight, knocking most of his opponents out. He had an on-going feud with the police, with whom he always seemed to be fighting. The peaked hat of a policeman was, to Jim, as good as a glove across the chops and the challenge to fight at dawn. He hated 'the boys in blue' with a vengeance. Jimmy, with his brother Dave, were the kingpins in rough Holbrooks, where even the police went around in threes – and that's in the station! When he was sober, which was not that often, Jimmy was a lovely man. But when he was drunk he became a ribald fighting demon, who would back down to no man. Very often he would end up fighting against whole gangs on his own, still coming out on top. He was the proverbial scrapyard dog. His thin, wan face was capped by short unkempt hair. His hard eyes said, 'fuck off,' no matter how you looked at them. His brother Dave told me once that they played a Sunday afternoon game of rugger with all the other lads from the local 'enter-at-your-own-risk' public house. The ball, for seventy-five per cent of the game, lay untouched in the middle of the pitch whilst the players had a free-for-all fight. Jimmy's team eventually won on account of the fact that their front runner was a brilliant burglar; they'd throw him the ball and tell him it was a video, and you wouldn't see him for dust.

Jimmy's second for the fight was to be his brother Dave, a huge man at six foot five and sixteen stone, ten of which was in his 'shovel hands'. He had an unnatural strength, almost a freak of nature. He once picked up a twenty stone man on the end of a builder's shovel.

Tony the Head's second was myself. Tony was working the door in Erections nightclub, Jimmy worked the Pink Parrot, so they arranged to meet and fight on the forthcoming Saturday night, after working hours.

Three a.m. Sunday Morning. The venue, Lady Herbert's Gardens. Then down into the Diplomat public house afterwards for a bevvie.

Jimmy and Tony had both been fit men, pugilists of good standing. But, with one thing and another, their fitness had dwindled over the years, and now neither had more than a good minute between them. Which, to be perfectly honest, is long enough in the arena that is three second fighting. This, however, was not three second fighting. It was match fighting which demands more than a minute's worth of breath.

They both had a week to find some sort of shape. In a week, all they found was how bad their shape was, and how stiff those fucking exercises made you. Both shared restless nights and moody quarrels with their loved ones. Both couldn't wait to get it over and done with. Tony's brow was etched with the memory of how powerful Jimmy's punches were from the last confrontation. Jimmy still had holes in his face from where Tony had bitten him. Both knew they were in for a hard time. Jimmy thought he'd take the title with his punching prowess and the fact that Tony was overweight. Tony thought he'd win because he was the heavier man and Jimmy was undernourished and unfit – his diet consisted of beer. Both knew each other's strengths and weaknesses. Sunday morning would tell.

Lady Herbert's Gardens lay almost hidden down a quaint side-street on the very edge of town called Chantey Place, cornered in by Cook Street, almost on the back doorstep of the once popular Coventry Theatre, now a bingo hall. Once the podium of top performers like Freddie Starr and Frankie Howerd, now holding stage to Fred Bloggs and the bingo caller, and a family of dancing balls. The gardens were surrounded in their entirety by a three foot high stone wall, greening with age. This was the garden of yesteryear's gentry; now it was home to the city's tramps and winos; Coventry's forgotten. Inside was a well-kept half-acre of splendid gardens.

I was to watch Tony's back, should things get out of hand. Dave was to do the same for Jimmy. It was one of the most awkward scenarios I have ever found myself in because I was a good friend of both fighters; really I didn't want to be there.

Half a dozen of the Parrot doormen came along to watch, all uniform in bulk and occupation.

The moonlight shone down on the pair as they squared off. The rest of us stood back by a red-brick summerhouse veiled in graffiti.

The tension grew to grotesque proportions as the two circled each other, the beauty of the gardens lost to this barbarous spectacle.

I felt a deep sadness inside me, watching two friends prepare to batter the fuck out of each other, but it had to be done, the rivalry between the pair had been building now for three years. This, they agreed, would be the final encounter – the last round.

Jimmy started the ball rolling by throwing a couple of stiff jabs that fell short of the target. Jimmy's guard was high. Tony's at half-mast. None of the spectators cheered or encouraged, all knew both parties and though they had greater loyalties to one side or another, all also had enough respect for both sides to keep quiet. Jimmy threw a jab/cross, connecting sharply with the cross on Tony's right cheekbone; this was the opening Tony was waiting for. He rushed forward as Jimmy's right recoiled, into grappling range, grabbing Jimmy hard and pushing him back several feet. He slammed three solid head butts into Jimmy's face then tucked his head away from Jimmy's short counter-punches. Jimmy seemed unperturbed by the butts, but his face gnarled with anger and exhaustion. Tony was also sucking in through orifices that he didn't even know he had. Half a minute into the fight and both men were flagging. So far it was an unusually clean fight, no biting or eye-gouging. Both fighters were showing the other a lot of respect. Still locked in a grappler's embrace by the Lady's stone wall, Tony whispered something inaudible to our ears and they both parted, moved back to the centre of the green ring and started again.

Jimmy shot out a stiff jab, then again a jab/cross, connecting, but not heavily. Again Tony, using his eight stone weight advantage, rushed forward, breaking down the distance and grabbing Jimmy, throwing him to the floor. Tony knew Jimmy was too good to box with, so opted every time for his strong point and Jimmy's weak: grappling distance.

As they landed on the wet grass, the wind hoofed out of Jimmy. Twenty stone is a lot of weight to have falling on top of you. Jimmy's fitness was bad, but his will was strong; he wouldn't give in, and he let Tony know by sinking his teeth into his cheek.

Tony just managed to pull his head away before Jimmy's jaws locked tight.

BANG!

He let him have another butt in the face.

Another deadlock. Jimmy couldn't get Tony off, but Tony couldn't finish Jimmy off. Again Tony whispered something to Jimmy and they stood up and squared off once more. This is pretty unusual in a street fight, I have to say. This kind of respect is rarely shown. Both were dying from exhaustion by now. Jimmy's face looked red and blotchy, Tony's the same, with his usually smart, side-parted hair hanging lankly in his face. Jimmy now lacked the stamina to take advantage of this fact. Jimmy threw a half-hearted jab, but lack of speed and fitness betrayed him and Tony, for the third time, sought the sanctuary of grappling range. They again fell heavily to the ground.

After a few seconds of embraced inactivity, Tony whispered something to Jimmy and for the last time the two tired, bedraggled men rose to their feet, shook hands and embraced, both glad that it was over.

The feud was dead and a strong friendship and respect was born. As is often the way. Both seemed disappointed with their own performances, some that watched also seemed disappointed. Myself, I knew that when two 'class' fighters get together they more often than not neutralise each other and the performance becomes lack lustre.

What I really admired was the courage of both to do it the man's way.

8. Love on the Door

I had loved working Busters, and probably, at one time, I'd have worked there for nothing. It was great. The people, the atmosphere, the music, the scantily-dressed, teasing beauties, the feeling of belonging, the camaraderie and K.T. Especially K.T. She only frequented the establishment a couple of times a week, but that was enough to keep me going. She never had set nights, so every night I worked was exciting, just waiting and hoping for her to arrive. Even a boring Monday became an exciting Saturday if she turned up, and time would go faster than a March hare on skates.

She was the most alluring, pretty creature, with a quiet, shy voice. She had a gorgeously pretty face with deep, sparkling eyes and shoulder length, corn-light hair. An ever-so-slight lisp in her voice made her seem both vulnerable and sexy. Petite, at five foot five (ish) with a firm, slight figure that was modestly veiled in a baggy white blouse and geni-slacks, that invitingly showed just the slightest hint of underwear. Just looking was heaven. She always arrived in a group of four or five of her student nurse friends, she too was a student nurse at Walsgrave Hospital.

Nurses, nurses, nurses. Just the name conjures up vivid pictures of figure-hugging uniforms and bed baths.

I must admit, I've got a thing for nurse's uniforms, but at thirteen stone, it's hard to get one to fit.

At first with K.T. it was just eye contact, then a casual 'hello', then, having broken the shell of her shyness, polite conversation. Quite often I'd offer to let her in the club free, mostly she declined, I liked her for that. The polite conversation grew to long talks and confiding revelations. I was going through a bad patch in my marriage at the time and someone to talk with was nice; not that I'm trying to justify what happened but sometimes you need a shoulder to cry on. Eventually I asked her, one night, for a slow dance at the end of the evening. She declined.

'You're married, it wouldn't be right,' she said quietly.

'You've got a boyfriend as well, K.T. I only want a dance, not to elope with you.'

At this, some four months after our first meeting, we shared an embrace that was as close as two people can be. We danced slowly, ever so slowly, to 'The Greatest Love of All', by Whitney Houston. Her firm, warm body moved ever closer in time with the music. My body tingled at the feeling of her body as it contoured my own. I felt the heat of her face as it touched mine, our lips met, her mouth opened invitingly, and we slowly, erotically kissed for the duration of the record. Our eyes closed, shutting out the world, closing our minds to the wrong we were doing, to the reality that would hit us hard at the end of a record that was etching itself into our minds. This moment was destined to stay forever as a beautiful memory, a memory to be recalled and recounted when over-powering, unwanted spouses nagged us into oblivion, or when life's mundane groove bored us senseless. A video to be played over and over again when existence became a stagnant pool of ordinariness.

The record did end. Our eyes met on the crowded dance floor for a second that seemed to last forever. Then she looked slowly and shyly to the floor, our embrace reluctantly broke and we parted.

'I think that was a beautiful dance,' she said quietly. Then paused for a second, wanting and at the same time not wanting to tell me what she was thinking. Knowing if she did, that it might lead on to greater things. A beautiful relationship it would be, she knew that, but it would be a delicate rose with the complication of many thorns. She dropped her eyes to the floor, hesitated.

'The rest of my thoughts are X-rated. I'd better go before I do something I regret,' she said sadly.

She walked off the dance floor and re-joined the company of her friends. I let her go though it was hard. The moment seemed too beautiful to spoil.

As she left the club, about fifteen minutes later, I tried to stop her, to speak to her, though I didn't know what I wanted to say. She had tears in her eyes as she gently pulled away from me, so I didn't give chase, but just stood amid a swamp of confused thoughts. One of her friends at the tail end of the leaving procession noticed my dismay, and stopped briefly to console me.

'Don't worry,' she said, 'she'll be all right.' I feigned a smile.

'Do you think it's wrong, you know, me and K.T.?' I asked, already knowing that it was. She sighed and shrugged her shoulders.

'I don't know what's right or wrong any more.'

At this she also left. I felt sad inside, yet happy and excited. The next few days found me in a world of my own, K.T. on my mind. 'The Greatest Love of All' seemed to be getting an awful lot of airplay on the radio. Thoughts of her stuck in my mind. My wife knew something was wrong, because I wasn't arguing as well as I usually did.

My work mates knew also, because I was working hard for a change. I told them I was just on a bit of a downer.

Monday, Tuesday and Wednesday went slower than a milk float with a flat. No K.T. Everybody else in the world and his dog came into Busters nightclub, but not her. I saw her friends and spoke to them. They just said she was busy. I gave one of the girls a copy of the extended version of Whitney Houston's 'The Greatest Love of All', and asked her to let K.T. have it. I hoped that she would try to contact me. By Friday it all became too much so I found out what number her room was at the hospital and visited her.

The nurse's home was newly built within the splendid Walsgrave Hospital, boasting a swimming pool, squash courts and tennis courts as well as leisure rooms and even a public bar on site for the staff. I believe it had a few odd rooms for sick people too! None of this, however, compensated for the very poor pay the people of this profession received. 'Angels' is absolutely the right word to describe the nurses, who are tireless and brilliant.

The nurse's home was a three-storeyed, L-shaped building that housed several hundred rooms for the nurses who came from far and wide. The building was modern with much glass. It was about four thirty on the Friday afternoon. I'd finished work a little early so as to pay K.T. a visit. I didn't know what kind of reception she would give me, perhaps, in the cold light of day, she might tell me to 'fuck off', maybe I had read this thing all wrong, or perhaps, as I hoped, she might fling her arms around me and welcome me. Either way I wanted to see her. My mind wouldn't rest until I had. I climbed the open plan staircase to the second-floor with baited anticipation. The smell of polished floors hung in my nostrils. What should I say? Would I be able to control myself if she was in her nurse's uniform? I doubted it very much, there's only so much a man can take. I pushed the thoughts out of my head and made my way down a well-lit corridor that had rooms to the left and right. 102. I stood outside. Damn it, even her room door looked sexy. I lifted my hand to knock, then paused and bit my lip. What should I say when she opened it? I lifted my hand again, opting to ad lib.

I knocked and stood back. No answer. I tried again, waited, still no answer. Just as I was about to knock for the third time, the door opened behind me. It was one of K.T.'s friends.

'Oh, hello,' she said. I was embarrassed.

'Hello.'

'She's gone to Southampton for the week, to see her parents.'

'Oh!' It was all I could muster.

'Do you want a pen and paper to leave her a note?'

What a good idea.

'Yes please. If you wouldn't mind, that'd be great.'

I can't remember what I wrote on the note exactly, but I do remember that it was committed and soppy. I didn't think I'd see her again anyway, so what the hell.

I slipped the note under her door, thanked her friend, and hastily left.

Back at the nightclub I still thought about her a lot. I had come to the conclusion, though, that I wouldn't see her again and in a way I was glad, I was married to a nice person, and although at that moment in time not happily, it wouldn't have been right.

The queue at the club was as big as ever, on this Wednesday night. I was searching people for weapons. Winston was to my left. I bent down to check the legs of the scruffy punk rocker in front of me for concealed weapons and the like. He was 'clean', though by the awful cartoon smell lines coming from him, not in a personal hygiene kind of way. Suddenly I caught a glimpse of her out of the corner of my eye, she was at the back of the queue with a few of her friends. She smiled shyly. I ushered her forward, completely ignoring everyone in front of me. She smiled and shook her head as she always did. I felt a surge of great excitement at seeing her. When she got to the front of the queue and inside the foyer, I took her by the hand and led her into the club, despite her quiet refusals. I could see that she was flattered, and her friends impressed. Her hand, warm and slightly shaky, made a feeble attempt to break free of mine. I gently squeezed it, holding it tight as I walked her to a corner so that we could speak in private.

The club was dark and heaving with revellers. I found somewhere to talk quietly.

'Did you get my note?'

'Yes,' she replied, shyly.

'I hope I never got you into trouble.'

'No, it's all right.'

'I meant everything I said in it.' She feigned a smile and sighed sadly.

'You're married, it's not fair.'

My eyes dropped.

'I know . . . I know,' I whispered quietly.

'I won't be coming here again. I only came tonight because . . . well . . . because! This is my last time. It's wrong.' She held my hand tightly. My heart sank at her words, though deep down I knew she was right, and knew it was wrong, and I loved her for her strength. She pulled away and disappeared into the busy club. I moped for the rest of the night and gave her a wide berth, trying to make it easy for her, and easier for me. At the very end of the evening, when everyone was leaving, K.T. lagged behind her friends a little as she walked past me. I gently linked her arm. I knew she wanted me to stop her.

'K.T., can I have a word with you before you go?' She gently pulled away from me.

'I've got to go, my friends are waiting.'

I could tell she wanted to stay, to be with me, but she knew that if she didn't go now and make a break from me, that she might never be strong enough to do so again. I pulled her back to me again. She looked so beautiful, so inviting and yet so unattainable.

'K.T., K.T.,' I said quietly and urgently, 'please hear me out.'

She stopped trying to pull away.

'I know it's wrong, me and you. And I know I'm never going to see you again. I can live with that, but I have to tell you before you go that I love you.' She stared up at me fiercely as though offended, and her beautiful eyes began to smart with tears.

'That's stupid,' she said, 'how can you talk about love? How can you love me?'

Her eyes began to stream, and I held her two shoulders tightly and looked deep into her eyes.

'I do love you, that's all I want you to know. I can live with never seeing you again, but not without telling you K.T., that I love you.'

I released my grip on her shoulders and she ran, crying, out of the club. I shook my head and my heart felt heavy; she was a beautiful girl.

That was the last time I saw her. Last I heard she was pregnant and about to get married to some lucky man. I hope that he appreciates her.

This episode happened during a particularly bad period before my divorce. In retrospect I know that I was wrong to fall for K.T. while I was still married, but as much as I can see it was wrong that it happened, I don't regret it. My encounter was brief, and never fully realised, but I did love K.T. and wherever she is now I wish her joy and happiness.

I still think about her.

9. Instant Karma

The Pippin looked almost regal, though out of place sat on the edge of the of the Ansty Road, looking not unlike a small stately home. Three steps led up to a dual-pillared porchway that had seen the ejection of many a disgruntled punter, usually bouncing off all three steps – if your aim was good – before coming to rest in the car park that was moated by a small nine inch perimeter wall. Opposite, front and side, were a few local shops and a petrol station.

The 'Pippin', as the locals called the pub, was sat precariously on the edge of the busy Ansty/Sewell and Hipswell highway crossroad, regularly the scene of 'amber gambler' accidents. Often the unfortunate crashes attracted not only a nosy crowd but also opportunist hot dog or quick-food vans eager to make a fast buck.

At that particular time the Pippin, according to reliable information from the managers, relief managers and bar-cellar men, was a hot potato of a pub that few landlords were willing to take on. Its reputation for violence frightened rather than attracted would-be tenants. The ones brave, or silly enough to climb aboard the Pippin had the luxury of virtually being able to name their own price to a brewery who were only too glad to pay up. The pub did attract many scallywags, crooks, fighters and vagabonds, but in reality it wasn't what I'd call a violent establishment, in fact, it was one of the nicest places I'd ever had the pleasure of working.

Due to its unpopularity with potential tenants and the aforementioned issue of acquiring suitable landlords, the brewery invariably placed relief managers in the pub almost by force. Nine times out of ten the relief managers were shitting themselves even before they set foot in the place. The next thing you know the punters are running the place; pouring their own drinks, demanding protection money and eventually attracting more people of the same ilk, until the place is an absolute shit-hole. And with each subsequent (weak) manager the reputation gets worse and worse.

The Potters Green Boys frequented the Pippin regularly and, though lords of trouble, they rarely put fist to face in the Pippin. They respected, or were scared of, the door team too much. There was around ten of them in all, aged between eighteen and twenty-two and at their violent prime – they rarely ended a night without a fight. As a rule of thumb it was them who picked it, generally with those they perceived to be weaker than themselves. 'Bullies' would be a good label for these people, though I find the word 'wanker' more fitting – if they happen to be reading this book I'll repeat that; 'WANKER!' just in case they missed it the first time. They were mostly young boxers, so they had a certain amount of physical ability, but their main claim to fame was their involvement/ties with the infamous Bell Green Boys. This association gave them, at least as they saw it, credence and their claim to fame. As one of the doorman at the Pippin I neither liked nor disliked them; they were tolerated.

The leather interior of the Granada Scorpio held Mr B's nine stone frame comfortably. The 2.9 injection 'dream machine' was, in 1988, the status symbol of every successful businessman. He smiled to himself as he cruised along the bottom of Hipswell Highway, Mozart dancing in his ears from his state-of-the-art stereo system.

He'd not long had the car so the novelty hadn't yet worn off. As he neared the junction with the Ansty Road the lights ahead changed to red and he began to slow, clipping his indicator on to 'right'. His intention was to head along the A4600 to the M69 and home, Earl Shilton, where his detached cottage in one acre of gardens held his heart, Helen. He'd rung her not long ago on the car phone to say that, at eight thirty p.m. he was on his way home. Her soft, educated voice held tones of 'missing you' that pleased him. Fifteen to twenty minutes and he'd be home.

Pulling up at the lights, he hardly noticed the six youths approaching the road from the right, preparing to cross. Mr B could not have known how violent the next few minutes were going to be, and how drastically they would change his life.

The Potters Green Boys had been on an 'all-dayer'. Eight thirty in the evening and they were already smashed out of their skulls, and why not, they were celebrating. Johnny, with his shaved, 'look-how-hard-I-am-and-what-a-twat-I-look' haircut, had just been released from the 'green' after serving six months for violence. As far as the 'Boys' were concerned, Johnny was the man now. All day he'd regaled them with the hardships of prison, and how stoically he'd handled it, and 'hey, it wasn't so bad, I'd do it all again'. They actually envied him and dreamed of 'doing time' themselves. In reality, Johnny cried like a baby for the first three weeks, even cried silently for his mother and crept and licked arses so much for the six months that the knees had worn out in his regulation prison trousers and his tongue was khaki-brown. At one point he'd even had to see the prison doctor for depression. The doctor took one look at his notes (he was serving time for a 'wounding' on an elderly man), and told him unsympathetically to 'pull yourself together'. He swore to himself there and then that when he came out, he'd go straight. He couldn't bear to be locked up again. The first day out he bumped into the lads, they treated him like a god, and after a couple of drinks in the Acorn pub, he started believing he was one. Now, several hours and uncountable bottles of Pils later, he was trying, with his followers, to get across Hipswell highway to the Pippin, if only this 'skinny cunt in the smart car would get out of his fucking way'.

I was stood on the steps of the Pippin with Dave, a fellow doorman, watching them as they approached the road. I sensed something bad was going to happen. I nudged Dave who was busy day dreaming and pointed over at the youths.

'Hey, Dave, they're gonna kick off.'

Dave followed my gaze; his hardy expression never changed. The 'Mars Bar' on the right side of his nose looked like a facial cleavage in the shadow of the early evening sun. He thought for a moment as though hedging a bet.

'Yep, I'd say you're right Geoff.'

'Those fucking wankers kill me, look at them, they've been on it all day.' I was already starting to get wound up.

Dave turned to me with a look of concern. He was about forty, an old school doorman who had long since deadened the emotional nerve endings of empathy. He could see that mine were still sensitive and raw.

'It's not your problem Geoff, let them get on with it. No one will thank you for your trouble.'

Johnny, with his very short, shaved blond hair, above a fat nose and narrow blue eyes, began to swear and cuss at the car and its driver. He did this for no other reason than it was there and he didn't think it should be. He was trying to live up to his image. Mr B inside looked visibly frightened. I left my podium on the pub steps and approached the perimeter wall, to get a better view, and assist if need be. Johnny started to kick the car and the cheering of his mates acted as a catalyst sending him into a frenzy. As he got round the car to the driver's side, they realised he was getting out of hand and tried to stop him. He was salivating as he screamed at the bewildered driver. He then punched his right fist clean through the driver's door window shattering the glass all over Mr B causing multiple cuts to his face, eyes and head. Somehow, even though he was being held back, he managed to drag the cowering Mr B from the car by his grey pinstripe jacket, hissing, spitting at him, and cursing. The ashen-faced businessman was splashed with his own blood, and in a state of shock. From my vantage-point he looked like a rag doll in the jaws of a large dog.

Technically, the situation was nothing to do with me, and as I edged forward toward the affray Dave told me so, and I hesitated. True, it wasn't actually happening on the grounds of the pub, but on the other hand an innocent man was being battered, and for what? For driving a Granada. I could have understood it had it been a Yugo. Johnny was pulling and punching Mr B and Johnny's friends were pulling him, but to no avail. He had somehow managed to drag his victim some hundred feet across the busy Ansty Road and on to the central grass reservation. The battering was merciless. The passing motorists seemed not to notice and carried on their merry way. All this had happened within seconds and I felt sick to the bone at the slaughter of this innocent man at the hands of this low life bastard. I could hear the ever-so-familiar sickly smack of fist on face and the involuntary grunts of the battered Mr B.

I had to do something. I couldn't stand it any more. I quickly ran across the road, careful to avoid the beeping cars. The anger was growing inside me. Dave shook his head; he couldn't understand why I was getting involved. It was an unwritten rule on the door that you never got involved in anything 'off the premises'. I couldn't help it though, I think I saw myself in that poor, innocent man, myself as a schoolboy, unable to fight my own battles and, like him, at the mercy of those stronger.

As I reached the debacle, the noise of violent cries, grunts and expletives rose high above the roar of the traffic. I managed to squeeze my hands through the mayhem of thrashing bodies and grab Johnny from the back. I put him into a rear chokehold and viciously ripped him off Mr B. I squeezed my choke hard across his throat. I felt like I wanted to break the fucker's neck. My choke forced a cackling noise from Johnny's throat as he gasped and snorted for air. He let go of the businessman and grabbed my arm to try to break the choke. I felt such a tremendous rage. I felt like killing him, destroying his being, thrashing him to within an inch of his life, as your dad might say. His friends still had a grip on him too.

Mr B slumped, semi-conscious on to the grass verge. He was in total shock. Due to the fact that Johnny's mates were trying to get a grip on him at the same time that I was trying to strangle the life out of him, I was failing to get quite the grip that I was looking for.

'Fucking get your hands off him,' I bellowed at them, and they all released their grip like he was on fire. Then I released mine. Johnny turned to me, half-crouched and holding his throat, gulping in air. My fists bunched in anger as he stood up straight and our eyes met.

'Right, you fucking wanker, let's go. Me and you,' I challenged. He thought about it, he wasn't sure. I took advantage of his hesitation.

'Fucking come on then, me and you. Go on. Just give me one excuse and I'll fucking level ya.'

I lined him up with my right hand, my adrenaline at fever pitch. He twitched as though forcing his redundant limbs to move. They refused; lack of moral fibre betrayed him. His mouth fell open in shock. He looked at his mates, then back at me. His bottle was going, and fast. I knew I had him, but should I batter him anyway, even though he obviously didn't want to fight me? Should I smash his consciousness into unconsciousness? Give him some of the stuff that he had so mercilessly dished out on Mr B?

'You fucking wanker,' I concluded, 'fuck off out of my face before I level you. Go on, fuck off.'

I was in my 'F' word phase. He scuttled off across the road, ashamed of his own cowardice. It was better really that I didn't hit him, if I did, he could have at least claimed to have 'had a go'. Better to send him away mentally defeated where excuses would hold no sanctuary for him. As Sun Tzu said in the art of war:

'Hence to fight and conquer in all your battles is not supreme excellence. Supreme excellence consists in breaking the enemy's resistance without fighting. Then with his forces intact he will dispute the mastery of the empire, and thus, without losing a man, his triumph will be complete, this is the method of attacking by stratagem.'

Or something like that!

His mates retreated to the pub and I helped a battered and bewildered Mr B back to his car. Diamonds of broken glass lay on the road and in the interior of his car. He couldn't even speak. I don't think he even realised who I was and what I'd done.

A loud shattering smash, then another, shot my head around to find the bearer of the noise. Johnny 'Bottleless' was smashing in all the shop fronts across the road with bricks and fists.

I watched as five young lads tried to walk past him. He ran at them challenging and cussing, but they were just nice young lads, not out for trouble. Understandably they ran away from him. Inside I smiled through my disgust. The act of smashing windows and challenging 'minnows' would not heal the burning from his seared ego. He'd lost his battle to me and nothing was going change that. He felt like a wanker, and so he should, he was one.

By the time the ambulance and police car arrived, Johnny had disappeared. The ambulance took the shocked businessman to hospital. The police followed the trail of broken glass. Johnny had smashed several house windows on route. With great difficulty they arrested him and took him to the cells. He got a measly nineteen months.

Mr B got much comfort from wife Helen when he finally arrived home from hospital. He cried in her arms. She knew what a sensitive man he was and couldn't comprehend why anyone would want to hurt him. He took a month to physically recover enough to return to work, but to this day still hasn't completely recovered mentally, always conscious of the beating and the possibility of another.

He found a new route home, a little off the beaten track and a little longer, but it by-passed Coventry and that made it a little safer.

10. Retribution

I think it's fair and true to say that, 'what goes around comes around'.

Peter was a B.A. Degree student in Leamington's Mid-Warwickshire College. At twenty he was in his second year and going strong.

Thin and wiry with a keen sense of fun and a zest for life, he'd become very popular with the other students at the much-populated college. He was one of four friends who frequented the nightspots in Leamington.

The first I knew of this affable young man was when I saw a feature about him on Central News. He was no longer fun-loving, no longer articulate. On the screen I watched his middle-aged mother and father, their sadness moving them to tears, help him walk through a Leamington park. His steps spasmodic, his mouth dribbling, his thin emaciated face pallid. Then the screams – they cut right through me.

This once fun-loving boy, the life and soul of the college parties, was a cabbage. No more youthful *badinage*, he couldn't speak, he couldn't eat or drink on his own. His life, to all intents and purposes, ended with the swing of a baseball bat in an unprovoked attack outside a Leamington nightclub.

As the story goes, the doormen who attacked him had the worst of a situation in the club they were paid to protect. In an attempt at retaliation, they armed themselves with bats and left the club to pursue their attackers. Apparently they were too late. Steve, the head doorman, was fuming and needed revenge. He knew he'd looked bad in the club and his ego was severely dented.

As fate would have it the three innocent students were walking past the nightclub on their way home just as the doormen exited with the bats. These students were not the men that had attacked them in the club; but they would do.

Steve, grizzly-faced and with shoulders like Goliath moved towards the young students with malice in his eyes. He needed any excuse. One of the students happened to be laughing.

'What the fuck are you laughing at?' he shouted. 'What's your fucking problem, what the fuck are you laughing at?'

The two other rather large doormen followed behind. Steve swung the bat menacingly in front of him. Not surprisingly Peter looked frightened and his fear locked him to the spot. He lifted his hands up in a capitulating manner.

'Look, we don't want any trouble, we're just walking past, just leave us alone, why . . .'

THUD!

People in the busy nightclub heard the crack of bat on skull above the beat of the music. Outside, everybody felt rather than heard the bludgeoning as the bat cracked open Peter's skull and he fell, unresponsive, into a puddle of his own blood. Everyone looked on in horror as an ever-expanding pool of blood swelled around Peter's head. For a long moment there was silence. One of Peter's frightened mates quickly fell to his knees at his side and frantically tried to revive him. Steve felt overwhelming panic. His partners in crime were equally dumbstruck.

'YOU'VE KILLED HIM, YOU'VE KILLED HIM, YOU'VE KILLED HIM!' Peter's friend shouted again and again.

Steve and the other doormen ran back in the club hoping to find a little sanctuary. Crowds of people leaving the club to find out what the horrific noise was met them. The ambulance men managed to save Peter's life, or what was left of it.

Steve and his fellow 'armed' doormen were finally tracked down by the police and, for their crime, were imprisoned for three years.

Peter has never recovered so I think it's safe to say that he got life.

Three years in a cell of steel and stone.

Life in a cell of flesh and bone.

The Central News feature was highlighting the case, and asked the questions: 'Why did it happen?' and 'Why were the sentences of the guilty three so lenient?' Three years in jail, out in twelve months with 'good behaviour', was hardly a fitting punishment.

The Pink Parrot nightclub in Coventry's city centre was probably the busiest and most popular of the clubs that the city accommodated. Certainly it was the newest, with spacious dance floors, ample bars, and snack counters upstairs and down. The club could hold a couple of thousand people, with twelve doormen to control the whole issue. Twelve may not seem many, but each of the twelve were veteran, named doormen under the auspices of Kev H, a gentleman, though very heavy in the city and further afield. A great leader of men, holding absolute respect from the doormen he captained, the management he worked for, and the 'punters' he looked after. He was a short, stocky, handsome pitbull of a man.

Steve and his mates were, I was reliably informed, in the club strutting their wares. They'd only been 'out' of prison a week, so were doing the rounds. There's something about a prison sentence that would appear to make the ex-cons think they're hard. When they 'go down' many of them are whimpering cowards, who can't fight sleep. Then suddenly, when they're released they miraculously become fighters, tougher than a Soho scrubber, men to be respected, men to be feared, and men to be looked up to.

OH REALLY? I don't think so. I think that they're the same people as they were when they went in except that now they've got a record and a right forearm like fucking Popeye – or a very close cellmate. Anyway, I never respected them, though I can't say I disliked them that much either. At that time I knew little of them other than the fact that they were doormen who had just been released from the 'green'.

We were alerted to the trouble by the sound of breaking glass, usually the first indication of trouble in a drinking establishment. We ran straight from reception into the busy club, which was filled to capacity with young, old, drunk, sober, thin, fat, smart, scruffy, pretty, handsome, ugly, smooching, dancing, drinking, joking people, all packed tightly into society's culture dish, the nightclub. Those who didn't move out of our way were (usually by accident) shoved out of our way as we raced to find the spanner in the works. On this occasion we didn't have to look far, it was happening just inside the club by the downstairs dance floor. Everyone stopped and looked on in fascination as we went about our duties, separating thrashing bodies. As I bent down to separate two violently embraced youths I felt a sharp thud, then a deep tingling sensation in my right eye. Some fucker had punched me from the side. At this point my head flipped and I knocked the perpetrator clean out with a right that exploded on to his chin. He lay unconscious amid a two dozen trouncing feet on a carpet that had seen more blood than a butcher's bench. He was out of the game before he even realised he was fully in it. Now I was incensed. My theory on separating fighting people is to do so with as little assault on them as is humanly possible. I wouldn't hit out or strike anyone unless the situation was beyond my restraining capabilities, or I got hit myself. I believe that if people are fighting in a club or pub, I, as a doorman, have no right to hit them for it, neither do I want to; I only want to eject them from the premises using a restraining hold with as little fuss as possible. Unless they hit me. My problem is that once I get hit, I lose it, and anything that moves after that is going to 'have some'. That may seem a little severe, it may seem like over-kill, but it's not, it's simply a matter of survival. Basically, the people you are dealing with, certainly as a doorman, make the rules, they dictate the pace. If they don't hit you, you don't hit them. However, if they do try to hit you, you have no choice (if you want to survive) but to hit them back. Once the first blow has been thrown at you or a fellow doorman you forget all about restraints and hit anything that isn't wearing a bow tie.

Stewart, one of the other doormen, a huge man at seventeen stone, had lifted my first K.O. off the floor by putting his hands under his armpits. He was dragging him like a sack of shit, out of the club.

'No, no, no!' Stewart shouted as I ran like a bull at the now consciousness-regaining man, and head butted him back to sleep. I ran at them so hard that I knocked them both over, and at the same time nearly knocking myself out. Instead of hitting his face with my head, I hit his head. I stood there for a few seconds and saw stars floating around in front of me. I felt a numbing sensation and had to shake my noggin to clear it. As my head cleared, another of the troublemakers made his play by squaring up to me. I dropped another nice right and he too hit the deck like a heavy thing. The other doormen had dragged most of the fighters from the club and I was faced with the last of the bunch: it was Steve, the doorman who had 'batted' poor Peter. He was clearly nervous of me – well, I had just K.O.ed his two underlings, one of them twice. I approached him menacingly, oblivious to all the people around me. No noise. Tunnel vision. Just him and me. We stood face to face. I wanted to hit him straight away, give him no chances. He was bad and didn't deserve a chance. I don't know if it was the bang on the head or perhaps I was in the 'zone', I don't know but I felt as though I was out of myself, as though I was standing by the side of my own body looking on. Top athletes tell me that this out-of-body experience happens to them at the height of their ability, where their bodies work themselves, finding the optimum movement for any given situation. It was a strange feeling of complete calmness, as though I knew I was going to do the right thing. Buddhists call it the state of no-mindness: 'into the soul, absolutely free from thoughts and emotion, even the tiger finds no room to insert its fierce claws.'

His body twitched, as though making a forward movement.

BANG!

I bludgeoned him into the lonely halls of unconsciousness. It was a sweet punch, though I say so myself. I heard the contact of knuckle on jaw, I also heard the thud as his unconscious body hit the deck, where it lay until the other doormen carried him from the club. They dumped him in the flowerbed just outside the doors where an ambulance collected him like yesterday's rubbish and transported him to a hospital bed at the Coventry and Warwick. A fractured skull kept him there for a week.

11. Robbery at Busters

J was the cheekiest bastard on God's earth, but I can't lie to you, I liked him. He was a crook, a fighter, a thief and a womaniser – those were his good points – but he was a very charismatic man.

My first meeting with the twenty-five-year-old was when he attempted a two a.m. robbery at Busters nightclub. I happened to be working there at the time.

J was a tall, lean, friendly fellow with a nose that had felt more leather than a cowboy's arse. He had tidy mid-cut, mousy hair, and an affable gait. He always had a beautiful girl on his arm and expensive clothes on his back. He walked with a bounding confidence that told you 'he'd been there'.

Saturday night, one fifty-nine a.m. and this popular nightclub was busy. Lush with people, noise, smells and atmosphere. Walking from the reception area to the bar through so many gyrating bodies could be a nightmare, and if you were carrying a drink, forget it. Busters was a wonderful nightclub moulded inside like a cave with a mini laser system that danced the revellers into a frenzy. The sunken dance floor was never free from sweaty, curvaceous ladies, and boys with 'desert disease' (wandering palms). The tiny D.J. box perched like an eagle's nest on the edge of the dance floor. This was usually manned by two D.J.s, the Asian brothers Dan and Wall Singh. Tonight though, we were honoured by the presence of Richard Barnes playing to the tastes of the day and scanning the club for trouble, or its potential. In the club, the D.J. was the eyes and ears of the doorman, any problems, no matter how small, and he would press the alarm. On the evening in question, at two a.m., the night's takings were busily being counted by Dave, the handsome, smart club manager, whose dark good looks attracted many an admiring glance from the ladies. These were always met with polite, unreceptive nods.

Dave was a very charming and charismatic man, but his tastes leant slightly to the left, if you know what I mean.

The small, cluttered manager's office was hooded in cigarette smoke. Dave, meticulously dressed in a grey suit, was counting the cash. Margaret, the lovely, bespectacled, pear-shaped middle-aged receptionist was watching over him. We (Colin 'No Neck' Maynard, 'Awesome' Anderson and Ricky 'Jabber' James) stood behind the glass doors that separated foyer from club, getting ready for the five-past-two a.m. rush for the cloakroom, taxi and home. The night had been relatively quiet with only the one bit of domestic trouble between a fat girl and her thin boyfriend who were quarrelling over her 'supposed' romantic glances at another boy, which ended in her waddling out of the club with him in hot pursuit. John and I were, as usual, wrestling around the tiny cluttered cloakroom. I was getting battered as usual. I was the only one brave or stupid enough to fight with him. Underneath his rather deceptive appearance lay biceps of about seventeen-and-a-half inches that had more crush than one of those fat snakes that I can't remember the name of. We had two cloakroom attendants ready to give out garments to the departing punters. One, a young Iranian student called 'Muhat

Mucoat', and the other, an elderly Scottish gentleman called Angus McOatup.

There was a steady hum of mingling voices in the background; the D.J. had stopped playing the music at two a.m. on the dot. This was very important if he valued his health. If he ran over – even by a minute – he'd have the doormen on his back. (Judging from the love bites on the back of one of our D.J.'s necks I figure he might have enjoyed this.)

A hysterical scream from the office stopped us at our play. It was Margaret. She screamed again. There was a commotion coming from the office. Myself and the other doorman stormed through the doors and into the office to save her from whatever it was that was causing her to scream so loudly. The sight that met us was J, with many, many bank notes sticking out of his bunched hands. Margaret and Dave were hanging from his frame like scarves. Within seconds we were on him like a second skin, holding him tightly so that he couldn't escape.

'All right lads, you've got me, it's a fair cop,' he said, 'just give me a few digs and let me go.'

All the doormen let go of him at once and looked at each other. It seemed like a reasonable deal to me.

'No,' said Dave indignantly, 'I'm going to call the police. I want this reported.'

We all shrugged our shoulders.

'Sorry mate, he's the boss,' I said.

'Aw, come on lads, you know the crack, give us a few digs and let me go, you don't need to involve the Law.' John gave him one of those 'don't fuck' looks. I'm sure that when John is finally laid to rest – not for a long time

I hope – his gravestone will read 'WHAT ARE YOU FUCKING LOOKING AT!?!'

'You 'erd what the man said, it's not our decision.'

Ricky; black, six foot four and a scary seventeen stone shook his head and spoke in his high-pitched voice, slurring slightly from hundreds of 'pro' boxing bouts.

'Hey man, you done the crime, you do the time.'

Colin, wider than his height, shook his head in disgust, he had taken it all rather personally.

'I think we should give you a dig and call the police. This is Busters, we've got a reputation to maintain.' He poked J in the chest to underline his message. Colin was like that.

Margaret, visibly flushed, called J a 'bloody bastard'. This was completely out of character and caused us all to turn around to look at her. This was the first time that she had ever openly come out on our side, she was forever 'calling' us for being 'too aggressive'. She and Colin had an on-going war of words always culminating with Colin on the losing end of a verbal battering.

At this, and realising there was no other option, J tried to flee from the office. Unfortunately, he ran straight into the doormen, or more specifically, into me.

BANG!

I dropped a right on his nose and it exploded. I didn't plan to do it, nor did I want to do it, it just happened. I automatically followed up – as one does – with a short right roundhouse kick that finished off what was left of his nose job.

Everybody 'oooed' in unison as the blow landed, except J, who cupped his hands over the broken nose catching the blood as it issued from the wound. He stood up and looked straight at me, then winked. Cheeky fucker.

'Nice one,' he said. Then he threw the cupped blood everywhere; over us, up the walls, on the desk, the chairs, and over Dave's lovely suit. Margaret screamed, Dave sat in his chair with a 'this really complicates matters' look on his face, and tried to wipe the blood off his clothes. J cupped more blood from his nose and rubbed it over his face. He ripped his own shirt open at the chest and ruffled up his hair. Ricky's mouth dropped agape. Colin's eyes nearly popped out of his head, I smiled. I really admired his spontaneity. John drew heavily on his cigarette.

In about thirty seconds, J, the affable opportunist thief, looked like he'd been machine-gunned.

We all looked on in helpless dismay as this clever, cheeky man threw himself into the corner of the room and shouted:

'Please, please, don't hit me no more, I've had enough!'

Everyone else in the room looked on, helplessly. John and I walked out in disgust, while Colin grabbed J by the bloody, ripped shirt, slung him into the leather-seated chair and slapped his face to calm him down. J smiled at Colin, he didn't need calming down. He knew exactly what he was doing; he was in complete control. The police were called.

In the half hour it took the police to arrive, J had banged his head and nose on the corner of the desk (ouch), and on the wall, had splattered more blood around the room, and had generally given himself a thorough beating. Colin slapped his face once or twice but besides that we never laid another glove on him, all the damage was self-inflicted.

'What the fuck are we gonna do with this man John? Why don't we just let him go – we don't need the police,' I said.

'It's not up to us Geoff, for me I'd give 'im a good dig and let him go. Dave wants the police involved; it's out of our hands.'

'Do you think that the police will fall for his ploy?'

'They're stupid enough.'

'What are we gonna tell them about 'ow he got the injuries?'

Rick and Colin walked in as I spoke.

'Tell them he done them himself, he did do most of them,' Colin said.

'No man, they won't believe that,' said Ricky

'Just tell them the truth, he ran at me and I 'it 'im in self-defence.'

The lads all looked at me. Colin laughed.

'I don't think the law of self-defence will stretch that far Geoff.'

'Yeah, but if we say 'e done the lot 'imself there's no way they're gonna believe us. I'll say I punched 'im and then 'e done the rest 'imself.'

Finally we agreed. The fact that he was robbing the place and that he did run at me should cover the fact that I hit him. Or at least I thought so.

As the police turned the handle of the office door to enter, J, sensing their arrival again, threw himself on to the floor in the corner of the room, and again pleaded for mercy from a bewildered Colin, who scratched his head in dismay.

The P.C. and W.P.C. tutted and shook their heads in disgust at the spectacle before them. They knew the crack.

J didn't care what they knew or how bad he looked. He knew that when the police statement was read out in court it would sound to the uninitiated like he'd been the victim of an unprovoked battering from four heavy-set bouncers. 'Bouncer' being the operative word.

J was a very smart man. In his statement he told the police that he'd walked into the office by mistake, confusing it with the gent's toilet which, coincidentally, lay directly opposite the office. He claimed that the doormen battered him for his mistake, making up the 'robbery' story to cover their (our) own backs. Of course the police didn't believe any of it but it wasn't for them to decide, it was for a jury in a court of law.

J was charged with attempted robbery and six months later was taken to Crown Court. We, the doormen, were ordered to appear as witnesses. As I've already said, I'd originally agreed with the lads to admit to hitting J in self-defence. But, after reading Margaret's statement to the police saying that none of the doormen hit J, I was forced to change my story and deny it also, or I'd make her look like a liar. So in court we had this innocent-looking 'robber' with multiple injuries telling the jury that he had been set upon, and us saying that all his injuries were self-inflicted.

The pine courtroom emanated polish and respectability. The twelve members of the jury looked down into the gallery with collective boredom. J looked smart, though still crooked, in his 'court' suit. Some people have a wedding suit that they only wear for weddings, others have funeral suits that they only wear for funerals, J had a court suit that he only wore for court cases. He'd walked these floors more times than the cleaner, so many times in fact that they were thinking of giving the lad a life membership.

The judge looked at us, the doormen, over his half-rimmed spectacles below the customary white wig.

'I put it to you, Mr Thompson,' said the patronising Lillywhite, defence lawyer, 'that you struck my client hard in the face and knocked him to the ground, whereupon you struck him again several times with your fists.'

'No,' I said evenly, 'all of his injuries were self-inflicted.' He shook his head demonstratively and looked at the jury for effect.

'And why, pray, would he want to do that?'

'Because he's a nutter,' I replied honestly.

The jury burst out laughing, then stopped when the judge shot them a disapproving glance. This particular judge was a tricky character, and had once sentenced a friend of mine to six months in prison for fighting.

'I could do six months standing on my head,' said my cocky friend.

'Then I'll add another three months on top, that'll give you time to get back on your feet again,' replied the judge.

In theory, J's feet shouldn't have touched the ground, but his defence lawyer was good. And then there was the M.D. giving evidence on his behalf. He talked about how he felt that J's injuries could not be self-inflicted.

He was an elderly man, a police surgeon with more letters after his name than there were wrinkles on his neck, and the jury loved him. He was educated and articulate, 'he must know what he's talking about', they thought.

Our story was basically factual; J attempted to steal money from the office and we caught him in the act. The part about him pounding himself against the desk and walls was also the truth. It was only the one bit about me hitting him that was erased from the story-line, for the reasons already mentioned. As I said, J's story was right out of a comic book.

'Money? Never saw none your honour.'

We said his broken nose was a result of him banging it off the desk.

J said we sat him in a chair and punched him till our hands hurt.

The M.D. said:

'The angle of the wound is not conducive with banging one's head in a downward motion on to a desk or table. It is more likely that the blow was delivered from above. I would say that the defendant was struck whilst seated by someone, who, at the time of the blow, was standing.'

If I were in the jury, I would have gone for it too. They loved it. It's *Quincy Jones* isn't it? The M.D. believed it too.

His theory on angular blows and their effect on the human anatomy (in this case the snoz) swung it for J and he got off. And fair play to him. The jury thought they'd done a wonderful job until the judge, as is customary after sentencing, read them J's long list of previous convictions for robbery, adding that he was due up in another courtroom in the same building that very day on another case of robbery.

They'd got it all wrong; they were as sick as pigs.

J looked as happy as a dog with two dicks. Myself and the other doormen were indifferent; we didn't want it to come to court in the first place. It just shows you how the law works though. Throughout the case it seemed more as if we were on trial than J. Still, I guess that's our fault for being bouncers and thugs hey? Still, in this trade that's the shade of light that you have to live under.

12. Death on the Door

You push it to the back of your mind. You try not to think about it. You avoid conversations on the matter and blank your ears when it's being talked about. You even close your eyes to the vignettes of death on T.V. pretending that it happens to others, but not to you. But, alas, in reality, the threat of death is a doorman's constant companion. It may only be on a subconscious level but it's there. It is his and his family's greatest worry.

A doorman is like a peacetime soldier, forever at death's mantle. Today he cuddles his children, tonight he grapples with fate, and you can't run from it, nor hide.

A servant saw death in the crowd of a busy Bombay market-place and he ran, fearing for his life. He begged his master for money so that he might escape Death to a place called Madras.

His master gave him money and a fast horse and he departed. The master, perturbed by his servant's dilemma, went to the Bombay market to seek out Death.

'Why have you frightened my servant?' he asked.

'Your servant should fear not,' replied Death, 'for I have no business in Bombay, my business is tomorrow with a man in Madras!'

Within five months in 1992 in Coventry, eight people were murdered, several others were maimed in shotgun, knife, and other armed attacks, and the way things were looking, there would be a lot more in the next few months. Mainly in the guise of 'revenge attacks'. I just hoped that when the shit hit the fan that I was not in the immediate vicinity.

In Coventry there are four main men, who have large, loyal followings. These four must, for obvious reasons, remain anonymous. All four of these men are good friends of mine, but, unfortunately, not good friends with each other. Over that violent year, all of these men, at one time or another, had fallen out with each other badly, causing mayhem and riots throughout the city, each coming back and counter coming back on each other in revenge attacks to prove a point. All, it would seem, fighting on the hill of power to become 'king' of the proverbial castle. At the moment of writing, the battle still ensues. When the bullets really start to fly (and I think it won't be long), there's a fair chance, because of the job I do and the friends I keep, that I'll be right in the middle of it all. There is no sense in complaining, life is a theatre of combat, and the sooner people realise it, and accept it and get on with it, the better. I will accept it, at least until fate deals me a better financial card and I can 'deal' out of the rat race and opt for a nice country cottage where I can live with my beautiful Sharon and write my books and plays and poems to my heart's content. I wait in hope.

Noel was nearly out of it too. So near that he could almost touch it, almost taste it. His life had been, in his twenty-three years, a hard one. Adopted as a half-cast child into a white family, growing up amid much prejudice and confusion, never quite finding a friendly bed on which to lie. Adversity, though, had made him strong, a fierce fighter.

His tall, muscular frame, long, curled Afro hair and handsome face put you more in mind of a male model than a pugilist. His fighting ability drew him to the door, though, like many doormen, he realised it was a mug's game and wished that he could do something else. The women groupies that seemed to hang around most doormen made the job bearable, and then there was Gus and Tracey, his employers at the underground student popular, Dog and Trumpet; he'd have worked for them for nothing. They treated him regally and gave him that sense of belonging that, up until then had eluded him. He loved Gus and Tracey like he loved life; they had filled a vacuum that he thought would always lie gaping like an open wound. Gus and Tracey loved him back just as much; nothing was too much for Noel.

The previous New Year, Noel had turned up on their doorstep sad and dejected, almost in tears.

'I had nowhere else to go,' he said. They welcomed him. He became one of the family.

Gus often spent more quality time with Noel than he did with his petite, pretty wife Tracey. And she, in turn, often spent more quality time with Noel than she did with Gus. Camaraderie, love, and a deep friendship had grown between the three. Noel knew, as did Gus and Tracey, that he was no longer just an employee, he was family. His thanks for their kindness and affection came in the guise of guard dog loyalty and a savage protectiveness of the pair. He never let anyone talk down to Gus and absolutely pounced on anyone who should so much as look crossways at Tracey.

Then there was Roy, Noel's partner and best friend on the door, who was handsome and rugged and a perfect partner in crime.

So much love, so many friends.

The one special girl in his life was Michelle. There were many female admirers in Noel's camp, but she was special. A pretty white South African lady who was a student of performing arts. It was ironic really, Noel was black and Michelle's family was white South African, and yet they loved him. He got on with the whole family famously, but then that wasn't unusual, he seemed to hit if off with everyone – unless people crossed him. Outside Busters nightclub I watched him knock out two opponents in an instant when they started on him; his hands were fast.

The Dog and Trumpet was an underground-warren type pub, in the middle of Coventry's city centre. By day it seconded as a popular eating establishment.

Friday, 23rd April 1992. The pub was as busy as ever, mainly with students from the local Poly. They loved 'the Dog' as the place was commonly called. They loved Noel and Roy too. The karaoke machine was playing, as usual, with many would-be artists – mostly piss artists – strutting their wares and singing their hearts out. Noel and Gus, much to everyone's delight, always finished the night singing a duet to Noel's favourite song, 'Endless Love'. Noel sang the girl's part with a surprisingly good voice, and Gus sang the man's part with an even more surprisingly good voice. It went down a bomb. By the time all of the punters had left it was twelve fifteen a.m., Saturday morning had just begun. Gus, Tracey, Roy and Noel sat around with many of the other staff for a quick drink and listened as Noel told excitedly of his changing fortune. He'd just had a portfolio made and had prospects of a modelling career ahead of him. Regular work with Gus and Tracey, good friends, a beautiful lady: life was sweet. They were all pleased for him. Things were coming together for Noel. He was happy.

'See you round, fat man,' he shouted jovially to Gus as he left the pub with Roy.

'Not if I see you first,' Gus shouted back, laughing.

They met up with Cam, Noel's close friend, who managed the Diplomat pub, and Marie, a friend of all three. They headed for the popular Pink Parrot. After a short spell they decided to head for B's nightclub to finish off what had been a good night.

Around two a.m. Roy was tired and decided to head for home. After a bit of play-fighting at the door of the club, Noel pushed Roy into the street and closed the door on him, laughing and joking that he was barred and couldn't come back in. After laughing at Noel's foolery Roy wandered off to the taxi rank.

The street that held B's was starting to get busy, many were making their way out of the nightclub to the taxi rank just up the road from the club, past a chip shop. Cam, Noel's tall, smooth-skinned, soft-spoken Asian friend, patted Noel on the back and said:

'I'm just going to run Marie and a couple of the others home. I'll be back in half an hour to pick you up.'

'OK. See you in a bit,' Noel replied. At this, Cam left.

At around about the same time, Wayne, a local D.J., was just across the road from B's, and about to climb into a black cab with his lady.

BANG!

An unprovoked punch pummelled into the back of his head sending a fuzzy feeling right through him. It was totally unexpected. His girlfriend jumped back and screamed.

Admittedly Wayne was a D.J., but that didn't mean that he couldn't look after himself. He turned and though still dazed from the blow, attacked back with a hefty right hook and knocked his attacker to the ground. In a panic, the taxi driver drove off leaving Wayne and his lady stranded, so they went back across the road to the club to call another. They were trying to work out why he had been attacked; apparently he was just there, which is reason enough for some people to feel as though they have to attack you. The taxi queue further up the road was far too long to wait in, and anyway, a few other lads were joining his attacker now, so he needed to get out of the way.

The scruffy, long-haired youth dragged himself from the ground much to the amusement of his mates. They mocked him on his defeat. By now there were a couple of hundred people in the street, and most giggled or stared as they passed him. His pride was throbbing like a hammered thumb so he ran across the road to the club to get his revenge on Wayne. The doormen at the front door of the club told him to fuck off before they gave him another dig.

'Fuck off you arse-holes,' was his reply.

The doormen dragged him into the tight reception of B's and gave him his second bashing of the night, then threw him back out on to the street. His mates, scruffy and arrogant, were not happy now and started to goad and barrack the doormen who answered by closing the door on them. Completely by coincidence Noel left the club at this exact second to look for Cam. He was still wearing his black and whites from his earlier stint at the Dog, and as far as the barracking lads across the road were concerned, he was a B's doorman. As one, they crossed over the road and surrounded him. Noel was oblivious to what had gone on.

'You carrying?' the leader of the group asked.

'No,' Noel replied, evenly splaying his arms, 'I don't need to carry.'

THUD!

Noel felt a dull thud, like a punch to his chest followed by a sharp and excruciating pain. In an instant, they were upon him thrashing and kicking. Noel had been stabbed through the heart. Everything else must have seemed like a dream; a myriad of thoughts and notions rushing through his mind. He plummeted to the floor only to be met by many frenzied, savage blows to his dying body.

It was over almost as soon as it started. No one could help Noel because it happened so quickly. His attackers fled into the night.

The flashing ambulance pulled up at the side of the road. People by the dozen were now looking on, some crying, some quietly and urgently chattering, most were dumbfounded. All were shocked. A cocktail of humming voices all speaking simultaneously, 'Is he all right?' 'Is he dead?' 'Who is it?' 'It's Noel. Oh no, it's Noel.' His body was urgently lifted on to a stretcher and the ambulance raced away leaving crowds of disbelieving people.

Unfortunately Noel Darcy died on the way to hospital. A single stab wound to his heart. He was twenty-three years old.

I'd never seen a dead body before. I went to the chapel of rest to see my first; it was Noel's. A small reception room was packed with doormen, friends and family, most were crying, some to distraction. A friend, a son, a boyfriend, a good man was gone. I was with Steve Cater, one of Coventry's veteran doormen. We'd both come to pay our respects. I walked into the chapel of rest with some trepidation, not quite knowing what to expect. Noel was laid out beautifully. We looked into the coffin – neither of us knew what to say. I hadn't known Noel as well as some but felt an affinity with a man that had walked the same dangerous path as I, and had paid the ultimate price. I touched his leg in a gesture of fondness, but the coldness made me shudder and I had to go. I made my excuses and left. At home I looked at those I loved around me and at my life in general and realised how lucky I was. It showed me that life was not a rehearsal – we could all be dead tomorrow and should make the best of every day, treating each as though it were our last. It may well be. It made me realise also that tomorrow is too late to say 'sorry', 'I love you'; too late to 'live life'; to change the job you hate so much; take the holiday that you've been meaning to take; to 'make amends', 'change', 'diet', 'train', 'have fun', whatever. Tomorrow may be too late. If there was one thing that I learned from Noel's death it was that life is precious and that not even one solitary second should be wasted on futility.

Our Lady of Assumption Church, Tile hill, Coventry.

The funeral of Noel Darcy was attended by hundreds of doormen, all dressed in the black and whites. Hundreds of mourning friends arrived from all over to pay tribute to this very personable man. Noel's closest friends acted as pallbearers and carried the coffin. The vicar said that he had never known such a well-attended funeral. It was a credit to Noel that so many people turned up to pay their last respects.

This chapter is a tribute to Noel, my friend and fellow doorman; and to Gus and Tracy and Noel's lovely family.

13. Part-Time Soldier
and other humorous encounters

In a sea of violence it is often the humorous moments that act as your metaphoric life-jacket, keeping you afloat when all around are sinking.

G, six foot three, sixteen stone of sinewy muscle and a cauliflower face, was everything that you might expect a doorman to be; gum-chewing, swaggering, protruding-chest arrogant. He was everything I tried not to be. He was on the wrong side of confident. G was a member of the T.A., which to people of his ilk was just an ego extension. It makes me smile that so many part-timers romanticise soldiering. I think that they forget that soldiers are there to kill people in times of war. This only usually becomes really obvious when a national conflict arises and their services are called for. During the Middle East conflict, for instance, many of the T.A. members – certainly the ones I knew – suddenly dropped out of the T.A. at a rate of knots with the 'bullet-in-the-foot-syndrome'. As soon as it became 'real' and there was a danger that the reserves 'might' be called up, most of them fell apart like cheap suits.

Actually I'm being a bit unkind; G was quite a handy lad, though I'd say that he had more front than he did bottle or ability. In a nutshell, G was a novice who thought himself a veteran.

He came into Busters one night with a couple of impressionable mates (also in the T.A., also left just as the Middle East conflict got started!). He was showing them around the town trying to impress them with what and who he knew. He did know quite a few of the lads so they were suitably impressed; that is until he pushed his luck a little too far.

A young lad and his equally juvenile lady were having a lover's tiff – actually she was battering him – by the crowded bar at the bottom end of this small but popular nightspot. The argument was getting a little out of hand so we the doormen intervened. Try as we might we couldn't stop the aggressive young female from shouting and threatening her rather coy boyfriend.

G had been watching from the bar only feet away, and in his wisdom, decided that the doormen were handling the situation all wrong. In an attempt at impressing his mates, and us, he decided to demonstrate just 'how it *should* be done'. Chest out, chewing gum to the beat of the music he swaggered across through the crowds of onlookers to the altercation. He had a lovely 'John Wayne' walk. Pushing his way through the crowds he placed himself right in front of the garrulous woman. She was a small girl at five foot with a six foot three attitude and a seven foot mouth. G faced her and, without provocation – without gesture, handshake, nod, wink, no 'please' nor 'thank you', no 'kiss my arse', nothing –

SLAP!

He just whacked her straight across the gob with the flat of his hand leaving a glowing red handprint on the side of her face. As his eyes turned to catch the acknowledgement of his mates, the toe of her high-heeled shoe sent his testicles into his stomach faster than a Porsche, and his heart, equally fast, into his mouth. For a second the only things that moved were his eyeballs; they crossed inwards, followed by his mouth, which dropped open. As the pain of 'crushed nuts' spread through his stomach he showed what he was made of by promptly collapsing to the floor. Everyone, with the exception of the young lady who was still trying to colanderise him with the toe of her shoe, fell about laughing.

When G finally found his shaky feet he walked, with a distinct crouch, back over to his mates who were having a hard time suppressing their laughter.

G's swagger had disappeared with his swallowed chewing gum and his chest had lost considerable inflation, somehow he didn't look so big any more. Needless to say, for that night anyway, G remained humbly quiet.

John 'Awesome' Anderson was looking on.

'Know what T.A. stands for Geoff?'

I shook my head.

'Total Arse-hole.'

I laughed until my stomach hurt the night that Barney and I ejected a 'woman possessed' from the same nightclub for fighting and being ugly. She was a troll.

Barney, so called because he was the double for a Barney Rubble character in the *Flintstones* cartoon, was a body-builder friend of mine. He was short with a heavy, powerful physique and a rugged face. He was the strong man on the Busters door.

The girl in question had just given some lad in the club a thorough beating so we'd asked her to kindly vacate the premises. Her unsolicited 'FUCK OFF' meant that we had to remove her forcefully, much to her dislike, and, my goodness, was she a handful. She kicked, punched, scratched and bit, she was like a rabid dog, and when I say that I don't mean any disrespect intended to rabid dogs. The whole screen was filled with knickers and torn tights (and that was just Barney and me). It was so undignified. Eventually we managed to throw her out. Now I know that to the reader this will all sound a little over-the-top. I know it will, because in your mind's eye you'll see two burly doorman getting physical with a dainty female. And if that were the case your concern would be warranted. But honestly she wasn't, not at all, she was a fucking scarer. The girl could model for horror posters, she really could. To be honest I don't think I could even describe her as a woman, in fact she wasn't even of the same species. Horrors like this are only found in the darkest corners of the 'nightclub jungle'. 'Why,' I often ask myself, 'are so many people wasting their time stalking the Yeti in Tibet and the Lochness monster in Scotland; come to Busters, it's full of them.' She was part-human part-beast.

Anyway, once the dirty deed was done we shut the red steel-reinforced door and locked her out – or ourselves in, depending on how you look at it. As soon as we had closed the door she started; she was kicking and punching at the door and shouting (unprintable names) at us.

I watched her carefully through the spy-hole in the door. She was a frightening sight. As soon as the abuse stopped and she moved away from the entrance I bravely swung open the door. She stared at me from about five feet away. I waggled my hips sexily and shouted:

'Heyee beast, I suppose a shag's out of the question?'

Well, what had I started? I felt terror run up and down my spine, exiting through my arse-hole. Her face contorted into a domino of hate making her previous ugliness tame by comparison. Barney reckoned she might have been wearing a Hallowe'en mask. (My answer was: 'No way! They don't make them that good!') Like a bullet from a gun she shot at me. Legs and arms flailing violently. She was a very heavy exploding Catherine wheel. I just managed to get myself inside and the doors shut, before she reached and devoured me. The reinforced door took the brunt of her onslaught.

By this stage, Barney and I couldn't speak for laughing. The more she attacked the door the more we laughed. Tears ran down my face in rivers and my stomach cramped. When we finally calmed down and the attack upon the door had ceased, I looked again through the spy-hole in the door to see if the coast was clear. It was, or at least it seemed to be. We creaked open the door, me at the front and Barney close behind, and peeped our heads carefully out. She was nowhere to be seen, so we slowly crept out like two night burglars, looking this way and that for the demonic damsel. Still no sign. I walked right out of the door with Barney sticking to me like a greased vest. I knew I was taking my life in my hands, but that's the kind of guy I am.

'Where is she?' I asked Barney. He shrugged his huge shoulders.

'I don't know, I can't see her.'

'Ha, we've obviously scared her off.'

'Are you sure?'

All the time that we spoke and scanned I could feel the uncontrollable urge to giggle rising in my stomach like a bad curry. There was no one in sight, only two lads about fifteen yards away to our right by the concrete staircase that led on to the roof-top car park above.

'YAAAAAAAA!'

The glass-breaking battle-cry deafened us, and we were temporarily rooted by fear to the very spot on which we stood. From her hiding place, crouched behind the two lads, she ran at us, like a Viking, stiletto in hand. Eyes wide in disbelief and mouths ajar with shock, in our haste and laughing hysterically, we turned, ran and tried to get back into the club.

The laws of expansion, not to be defied, said 'fuck off' and wouldn't let both Barney and I through the door at the same time, no matter what the danger. All the time that we struggled to get through the door she was getting closer, and I could almost feel her breath on the back of my neck. My hair stood on end, and a cold shiver ran down my spine. Eventually, after what seemed like a lifetime, we managed to squeeze through, falling on to the floor with Barney on top of me, both crying with laughter as the door took a third pasting.

She did eventually 'go away' when Colin cooled her down with the fire extinguisher. I half expected her to melt like the 'Wicked Witch of the East' from *The Wizard of Oz*. I was only glad that we didn't have to fight her, I'm sure we would have lost.

A lot of people like to take cheap shots and throw down verbal gauntlets. When you're a soft-spoken, mild-mannered (damn good-looking) fellow with an ever-so-slightly receding hairline (so slight that you might not even notice), you sort of expect it. Few of these antagonists see the funny side though when you retaliate. The two disillusioned lads from neighbouring Rugby proved to be no exception. When they threw down the gauntlet and I picked it up and tossed it back, they were no fun at all.

Both were tall and skinny, one had a thin, gaunt face and 'hand-me-down' apparel, the other a frowning, aggressive face and staring eyes.

The two left Busters well before the end of the evening. Colin 'No Neck' and I were stood, minding our own business, by the exit door as they passed on their way out. Neither of them were happy and thought they'd tell us why. We weren't really interested but they told us anyway.

'We're from Rugby,' said the gaunt one, 'we came to Busters tonight to have a good time but we've had a crap night and it's all because this is a shit nightclub, in a shit city, and we won't be back again!'

He poked aggressively at my chest to add emphasis.

I was annoyed at his disrespectful and insulting manner.

'Why don't you fuck off back to Rugby then?'

I like to try the polite approach first.

'It's only a one horse town,' I continued, 'and hey, you'd better hurry, they shut the gates and turn the lights off at twelve o'clock.' Colin laughed but the country yokels were not so amused.

'It's a lot better than this shit-hole,' the gaunt one replied bitterly.

I could tell that he was beginning to bite so, sure that I was on a home run I struck again.

'Listen mate, there are only two things that ever come out of Rugby, steers and queers, and I don't see any horns on you.'

He thought for a moment about the implication, then when the penny dropped he started cursing and swearing at me. I laughed. After a few seconds, and feeling vindicated, he and his 'jumble sale' friend turned and began walking away.

'I'll be back for you, you wanker!' he concluded. I should have just let them go really, but I couldn't, especially with Colin spurring me on.

'Hey mate.' As I shouted they both turned around. 'Isn't your mother the local prostitute in Rugby?' A cheap shot, I know, but I couldn't resist. He turned red and then green, he got so angry that he was struggling to get his words out. I thought I might have hit a nerve. Frustrated at his verbal incompetence he resorted to the obvious and ran at me fists ablazing – only to be stopped by his mate who dived on top of him and forcefully held him back. I know I was very lucky.

Colin and I burst out laughing. This just made him worse. He was almost foaming at the mouth by now and his eyes were trying to exit their sockets. His companion wrapped himself, like a blanket, around him until, finally, he calmed down. When he was calm his mate persuaded him to 'leave it'. They turned and began to walk away.

'I'll be back you bastard, I'll have my day with you, you'll regret ever crossing me.'

His attack was at me and I saw no point in trying to keep on his good side if he was going to get all mardy with me. I went in for the kill. I placed my thumb and forefinger to my mouth, mimicking deep thought, and said:

'Hey, it's your dad that's the pimp, isn't it?'

Oh my goodness, what had I done? This really upset him, he turned all the colours of the rainbow and ran at me again like a man possessed. This time his friend had to practically fight with him to stop his one-man crusade. My belly ached from laughing at the spectacle before me.

'YOU BASTARD! I'VE LOST *BOTH* MY PARENTS!'

Well now, *that* was a stupid thing to say. A very valuable piece of information that he would have done well to keep to himself. Colin looked at me and then at the man from Rugby.

'Well! Losing one is bad enough,' he said dryly, 'but losing two, well that's just downright careless.'

'Yeah,' I added, 'but don't worry, you're bound to find them when you're cleaning up, they're probably down the back of the settee.'

'AAAARRRRRRRGGHHHH! YOU BASTARDS!'

Now he was really angry. I can spot these things. He was so mad now that he foamed at the mouth. He tried to wrestle free from his mate to get at us. His mate was getting a little fed up with trying to hold him back.

'Fuck it!' he shouted, letting the brothel-keeper's son go. 'If you want to fight with him, do it, I'm sick of trying to hold you back.'

At this he tried to rush froward at me but to no avail. Lack of moral fibre had glued his feet to the spot. His bottle had left him via the back door. He had just discovered that adrenaline was brown.

'Come on then, what's the matter with you? Your mate's not holding you back any more.' I knew he wouldn't fight.

'I'll come back another time, I won't forget this.'

'Yeah, sure, I'll be waiting, ask for me by name, it's Geoff Thompson.' He nodded his head, as these people do, and disappeared up his own arse-hole. Really, these people shouldn't go for the title. I have a lot of experience in these matters. I can tear people to shreds when they start. Really. I'm an expert in these matters.

My hair – or lack thereof – has always been a source of mock and ridicule for potential antagonists, something that I've had to learn to live with – or, in fact, live without. I'm not sure whether the people that feel they have to mention it really mean it as a direct insult or not, though when someone calls you a 'baldy bastard' it's not easy to take it any other way. I have learnt over the years to weather these insults and also to expertly counter them when the opportunity presents itself. It annoys me though, when the gauntlet-throwers respond negatively to my 'counters' (usually in reference to their 'warts' or fat hips), after all, it was them who started it. People love to be smart and give it out but none seem keen to 'take it'. Some though, are a little too quick for me to get back at. One night I'd thrown a lad out of the nightclub for being ugly and scaring the women (I'm joking, he was stealing handbags). He proceeded to walk a safe distance from the door and in front of a large and appreciative crowd shouted:

'OI! BALDY! DIDN'T ANYONE TELL YOU THAT RECEDING HAIRLINES ARE OUT?'

Even I had to laugh at his cheek.

A particularly stout man who was bigger than a pie shop passed me on his exit from the nightclub, trailing two stone of buttocks. He had two pretty ladies on his arm that he thought he might impress at my expense.

'Hey chap,' he quipped, pointing at my depleting hairline, 'you want to have a word with your hairdresser.'

'And you want to have a word with your dietician you fat bastard,' I quickly responded. He coloured up and his two lady friends went into fits of laughter.

'What a blow-out!' one of them said through gulps of laughter as the fat man beat a hasty exit.

I can also clearly remember, as though it were yesterday, the smarmy woman who tried a similar dirty trick in a bid to gain a cheap laugh with her friends, again at my expense. Now, I don't mind people having a laugh at my expense if it stays within the realms of good taste or, alternatively, if I know them, but when complete strangers feel compelled to insult me I find it disrespectful and I do take offence. On this particular occasion I was working at the Diplomat pub in Coventry city centre. It was near the end of the evening and I was politely asking people to see their drinks off. I approached a group of about half a dozen lads and ladies, and in a voice that would have made Ghandi sound aggressive I asked them would they mind drinking up as it was time for us to close. Myself and my request were blanked completely. The aforementioned 'ugly bitch' who was a member of the group and not happy enough with the fact that they had already totally ignored me, thought she'd add her two penneth worth. She looked me up and down patronisingly, then looked at my head. She pondered for a second then announced to me and the people who were in hearing range:

'You're losing your hair!'

I felt embarrassed to be honest, though I didn't let her see. All the same my honour needed defending so I 'defended' in the only way I knew how.

'It could be worse,' I replied, looking her up and down like a she was a bag of shit. 'I could be about three stone overweight!' The whole group went deathly silent. 'And if you're so concerned about my lack of hair how about donating a bit from the top of your lip?'

She went very quiet. I walked away before she could think of an even smarter reply. Of course I know that sounds a little impolite, but people in glass houses shouldn't throw stones.

Drunken women, and I mean no offence when I say this, are the very worst when it comes to taking cheap shots, telling you as a matter of fact what they think of you or parts of your anatomy, and in my case it's the dreaded receding hairline. I always, always, have the last laugh on these people with my uncanny knack of hitting nerves with sharp, wicked counters.

'Good-night fat arse!' is a particular favourite, as they leave the pub at the end of the evening or:

'There's no need to take it out on me just because you're flat-chested!'

Or even:

'You smell nice. Have you been sick?'

I'm not a naturally vindictive person. I've had to practice very hard to get this good. But when people verbally attack me for no reason and with the sole intention of embarrassing me, then I will let go, verbally, with no holds barred. Believe me, it hurts them a lot more than it does me. Women, especially, hate being reminded of cellulite, flat chests, big noses, moustaches etc. But, if they insist on reminding me of my lack of hair then I feel obliged to dispense a few home truths in retaliation. It's only fair.

I've always admired wit and certainly it does seem to be a by-product of working in the 'people business'. Though the humour is often very black. The best stuff is anyway. One doorman I knew even carried his wit into the county court with him. He'd just been sentenced to six months in prison for a fighting offence.

'Have you anything to say?' asked the sour-mouthed judge.

Cool as you like, Mr Wit reached into his inside jacket pocket and casually removed a silver cigarette case, flicked it open, raised it to his mouth and spoke into it in an exaggerated American accent:

'Beam me up Scotty!'

The whole courtroom, barring of course the judge who remained stony-faced, flared up in a crescendo of laughter. For his cheek the judge added a further eight weeks on to the end of his sentence. A small price to pay, I think, for such a classic show of brave wit.

Epilogue I

Today, 15th June 1992, as coincidence would have it, *Watch My Back - A Bouncer's Story*, goes to print, just as I have finished the last chapter of the sequel, *Bouncer*. If people are kind, interested or curious enough to buy *Watch My Back* and it's a commercial success, then this book should hopefully follow in its footsteps to the publishers, printers and bookshops. If *Watch My Back* does not succeed, then this will probably by-pass all three on its way to my bedroom shelf, where I'll no doubt give it an annual dusting-down and talk about the time that I nearly became a writer. I pray that it's the former rather than the latter.

At the time of writing this book I am still working on the Devon door under the auspices of the charismatic Seymour, a gentleman/fighter of great standing. In the day I am conscientiously trying to earn my living as a writer. Still in my beautiful little house, with my beautiful Sharon, who is behind me one hundred per cent. I've said it for the last six months and I'll say it again now. Nineteen-ninety-two is my year, I believe this year will bring me success in some shape or form. Happiness I don't seek, because I have it by the barrow-load and I thank God for it. I love God. He has given me Sharon and my four beautiful children, Kerry (fourteen), Lisa (twelve), Jennie (nine), and beautiful Louis (three), (named after Joe Louis the boxer), and more chances than I have deserved. Credit where it's due, thank you God.

Epilogue II

It is now July 1999. Violence is increasing in society, though in my own life it is becoming a much smaller part. Eventually I want it to take no part at all. I hate it. I am embarrassed that it has been such a big part of my life for so long. It is a very low and unintelligent form of communication. Sometimes when I read over my books I don't see myself looking back from the pages of the past. Rather I see a fucking Neanderthal. Someone with a small intellect and a big right hook. It was what I always thought I wanted of myself; to be a fighter. Now I realise that I set my sights very low indeed. It is not what I wanted at all. So now that I am there, as a fighter I am choosing better. I am choosing to place all my energy that thus far has been misappropriated, into a more worthy goal. I am going to be a world-class writer. But now that I am where I thought I wanted to be (realising that I am at the wrong locale) I find myself struggling to be free from the physical security that I have built around me. I am scared to let go of the violence. Scared, I think, of being a bullied child again. A weakling. Given time though, I shall move on. The first step at this point in time will be to give up the door. From there I will be gentle with myself and wean myself off this drug. But I am not unhappy that I experienced it. In fact, I'd go as far as to say that without experiencing violence I would never have been able to grow beyond it. I am what I am because of the door. Without it I would have never made anything of my life, I am sure of that. Sometimes you have to go through something to get past it. As a doorman I learned how to administer violence as brutally as is needed. I also learned how to become the type of person I used to despise, without even realising it. The bullied child who stood up for himself became the bully. But now, having renounced violence, I have learnt the art of fighting without fighting.

I smile when I watch the romanticised film violence because they make it look easy when really it is extremely hard. They make it look fun when really it scares the crap out of you. They also make it seem right when even an idiot can see that it is patently wrong. And though most don't like to admit it, the films make you want to be there, they make you feel like getting your hands dirty with a little violence. In reality, and in all honesty, when it happens to you, it is the last place on earth you want to be. What we think it's like and what it actually is are two completely different things.

Involvement in extreme violence has, at times, made me doubt my sanity. Sleeping, eating and drinking the stuff as a way of life and thinking the kind of ugly thoughts that should never enter the mind of any rational person has really made me question who I am and what I am about. It has forced me to be introspective, to go inside myself – and oh what a fucking mess I have found. But that's OK, at least I now know it's a mess and can start to tidy up a little. Get rid of the repressed crap that has created a lot of my insecurity and violence, the shadows that have taken away my light for so long.

I write about all these stories because they happened to me, and not to promote violence. Actually, it was in the writing that I first started to realise how wrong it all was. The stories are true. I try not to colour them at all. I am hoping that others might read and think, 'that's something I never want to experience.'

Enlightenment as developed by facing extreme adversity has enabled me to attain a polarised personality. Now, looking ahead, I hope the experience will enable me to set my sights even higher, to climb even greater Everests.

Thanks for reading *Bouncer*.